DARKLY

DARKLY:

BLACK HISTORY AND AMERICA'S GOTHIC SOUL

Leila Taylor

Published by Repeater Books
An imprint of Watkins Media Ltd

Unit 11 Shepperton House
89-93 Shepperton Road
London
N1 3DF
United Kingdom
www.repeaterbooks.com
A Repeater Books paperback original 2019
3

Distributed in the United States by Random House, Inc.,
New York.

ISBN: 9781912248544
Ebook ISBN: 9781912248551

Printed and bound in the United Kingdom by TJ Books Ltd

Dedicated to
Rita Megerle, Joan Newby, and Joyce Taylor

Within the Veil he was born, said I; and there within
shall he live, — a Negro and a Negro's son...
Blame me not if I see the world thus darkly through the
Veil, — and my soul whispers ever to me, saying,
"Not dead, not dead, but escaped; not bond, but free."
— W.E.B. Du Bois,
"Of the Passing of the First-Born",
The Souls of Black Folk

Call me a bruise, but I can't have black without a
little bit of blue.
— Dazia

CONTENTS

GOTH-ISH

Goths reject the bourgeois sense of human identity as a serious business, stable, abiding and continuous, requiring the assertion of one true cohesive inner self as proof of health and good citizenry. Instead goths celebrate human identity as an improvised performance, discontinuous and incessantly re-devised by stylized acts. They like carefully staged extremism, and vicarious or strictly ritualized experiences of the dreadful Other.

— Richard Davenport-Hines, *Gothic: Four Hundred Years of Excess, Horror, Evil and Ruin*

If the funny T-shirt slogans and crisp khaki pants of the average American tell the lie that everything's going to be OK, the black lace garbs and ghoulish capes of goth tell the truth — that you suffer, then you die.

— Sarah Vowell, *"American Goth", This American Life*

The brochure from the New Orleans Haunted History Tour company promised a "leisurely daytime stroll through St. Louis Cemetery #1." I'd been on the French Quarter tour that ended with Hurricane's at Lafitte's Blacksmith Shop, where a pirate from the 1700s hung out in the back corner. I'd been on the house tour where the ghost of a love-stricken octoroon woman froze to death on a hotel roof waiting for her French lover who would never come. I'd been on the vampire tour that was similar to the others only with more references to Anne Rice. They all tell the same stories in slightly different ways, but this particular tour guide had an agenda.

I was expecting to see houses where ghosts could be spotted in windows on dark nights, or corners where someone was horribly murdered decades ago, but instead the guide, who was Black, herded his group of white tourists (and me) past Congo Square, the park which in the 1800s was the one place where Africans were allowed to congregate freely. He told us about the system of plaçage, a quasi-civil-union between European men and Black[1] women that allowed their children an inheritance. We walked past Tremé and he told us about Storyville and jazz and showed us a map of where we were in relation to the Lower 9th ward, the mostly Black neighborhood that suffered the most from Hurricane Katrina. When we finally arrived at St. Louis Cemetery #1, he showed us the grave of Vodou queen Marie Laveau, where tourists scrawl X's in groups of three on her tomb. He reminded us that her power was less about the supernatural and more about her access to the wealthy and connected. He pointed out the grave of Homer Plessy, of the landmark Plessy v. Ferguson case that said segregation was perfectly legal and which opened up the floodgates for Jim Crow.

While I could have used a few more ghost stories, I got a kick out of this unexpected tour of Black New Orleans history, but when I looked around the group everyone else looked bored and a little annoyed that they were not getting what they paid for. But it *was* a ghost tour, just not the kind they were expecting. These weren't poltergeists and spirits trapped in hotels, bars, and brothels, these were the ghosts of our history, the spectral remnants of our nation that were too often forgotten and dismissed. We were all hoping to be a little bit frightened, to stand in the spots between the past and the present where the veil between the living and the dead was at its thinnest. We were expecting to be entertained by macabre tales with a patina of historical truth. But as the tour guide understood, America's haunted history is Black history. At the end he suggested we visit the Museum of Free People of Color and I gave him a $5 tip.

I Am Darkness

My name is Leila, pronounced "lee-lah," which is not the way most people pronounce it. In Arabic, it means "night" or "darkness" or "dark beauty." I asked my father once where the name came from, why my parents chose a name so much more exotic for me than my siblings Jeff and Leslie:

He said, "It's your name."
"Yeah, I know, but where did it come from? Why did you pick it?"
"You were born, and it was just you."
Whatever.

I never got an answer to my question, but I quite like the idea of me emerging from my mother's womb and handing my dad a calling card reading I AM THE NIGHT in black-letter. It makes my morbid predilections inevitable, genetic even — a predisposition to horror movies, black nail polish and a preference for the Cure. I was destined to smoke clove cigarettes and write bad poetry under bridges in the rain. I am Darkness.

Even my birthday was shrouded in supernatural mystique. According to family lore, the obstetrician told my mother that she was carrying a boy due in April. Perhaps they were unsatisfied with that answer, so she and my sister asked Ouija for a second opinion. The talking board spelled out G.I.R.L. (which I am) and M.A.R.C.H.2.8. (I was born on 29 March). Close enough.

As a youth, I would say I had two main influences: Siouxsie Sioux, lead singer of the post-punk band Siouxsie and the Banshees, and Denise Huxtable, the fictional daughter of Cliff and Claire Huxtable on *The Cosby Show*. Siouxsie and the Banshees were the musical equivalent of the macabre, nightmares I could dance to, and Siouxsie Sioux represented a kind of dark glamor that I appreciated — a femininity that eschewed pink and politeness. She never seemed to smile, and I appreciated that. But Siouxsie was never aspirational for me, my idolatry stopped at the music and the Cleopatra eye shadow. I loved Siouxsie and the Banshees, but I wanted to BE Denise Huxtable. With her layers and layers of oversized clothes, floppy hats, and her fabulously mutable hair, she exuded an alternative New York City cool that I could only try my best to emulate. Her voice sounded like mine, her parents were like my parents — they were professional (my dad is an architect and my mother an anthropologist) and listened to jazz. She was smart, creative, and, like me, the family's designated weirdo. She sometimes got into trouble, but like me, she was ultimately a good kid. Denise didn't have a vaguely offensive pseudonym and never wore a swastika as a symbol of rebellion, and the worst thing she ever did was get a D on an English paper. Her life seemed attainable, and most of all, I *looked* like her. Siouxsie represented how I felt on the inside and Denise was who I could be on the outside.

Like teenagers everywhere, the walls of my room were a gallery dedicated to the music I loved, an environmental mood board of maudlin teen angst. I didn't have to talk about my feelings; the poster for Joy Division's *Closer* did it for me. I surrounded myself with a collage of white faces and spikey hair immaculately torn from *The Face, Interview,* and *i-D* magazines, and I would bend the spines as far as they would go until the pages could be plucked out neatly and intact. There were black-and-white Xeroxed copies of Caravaggios overlapped with pale blue concert ticket stubs, and photos of gothic spires and tombstones from Highgate and Père Lachaise cemeteries. There were snapshots of my friends posed dramatically in the archways of the Detroit Institute of Art with way, way, way too much eyeliner, blood-red lipstick, and frantically teased up hair like Robert Smith. I'd look at the photos of my idols in *Smash Hits* and my white friends with their vampiric pale skin, and I will admit that I was sometimes envious at how effortlessly they could *present* as goth. Mark Fisher called Siouxsie's look a "replicable cosmetic mask, a form of white tribalism." I never wanted to be white. Whiteness was never something I aspired to, but I considered myself a member of this tribe, and that mask never fit me. I'll admit, I sometimes felt a bit *Blacula*-ish in their presence — a Black version of a white story.

Still life with Bauhaus on window sill, photo by L. Taylor

One evening, my dad knocked on my bedroom door. "Hey, kiddo," he said looking around at my walls plastered with white faces. His eyes landed on a photo of a Black woman — a close-up of her face looking right into the camera, high contrast black-and-white, her head shaved. He said, "Is that your token black person?" with a breezy laugh, told me dinner was ready and left. A whole new kind of shame came over me, and days and even years later I would wonder if maybe I did only put that picture up because of some deep-seated guilt that I was betraying my race, that I was overcompensating for some unconscious desire to be white. The model wasn't just Black; she had a defiantly dark Black face, three shades darker than mine. I thought a bit meekly, "I just thought it was a cool photo," but now her dark eyes followed me across the room in stoic judgment, so I reluctantly taped up a photo of Terence Trent D'Arby.

I grew up in Detroit and there are few cities in America as unequivocally Black. According to the 2010 census, Detroit is the Blackest city in the country, with almost 83% of the population identifying as African American. I went to a very small Quaker school where the students were Black (mostly Black), white, Indian, Asian, and Middle Eastern. There were Christians, Jews, Hindus, and a few actual Quakers. There were rich kids from Grosse Pointe and poor kids from the Black Bottom neighborhood, and kids like me from Boston-Edison whose families lingered in the economic middle. Sometimes we dipped a little lower. It was a somewhat bougie, NPR type of upbringing and my cousins in the suburbs and my Black friends had similarly comfortable lives. I took classical guitar lessons, rented arthouse movies and read Sartre well before I could understand it. In the summers, I spent my days at Heritage House, a multi-culti enclave where I took African dance classes and learned about my "culture" in a large, redbrick Victorian House with polished wood floors and stained glass windows.

Then there was the summer when I was sent to the YWCA day camp downtown where I had lessons in swimming and social ostracization. It was in "the hood" and the girls terrified me. They banded together in cliques and looked at me from across the room, side-eyes full of the bitter judgment that only a group of preteen girls can invoke. They got into fights, real physical fights, not the psychological warfare typical of the cool girls at Friends. It was the first time I was called an "Oreo" and made fun of for talking white and acting rich (I thought to myself, if my family is rich why am I at the same shitty Y as you guys?).

They listened to New Edition instead of Depeche Mode and we might as well have been speaking two different languages, so I spent the summer with my head down and my mouth shut. It was my first experience of a culture shock within my own culture, and again I was assessed that my Blackness was somehow not Black enough, that I listened to the wrong music and liked the wrong things, and I was hit with a commodified identity crisis in which the things I consumed were indicative of my class and race. Before, the clothes I wore, the posters on my wall and the albums I listened to, categorized me as a person who liked a particular kind of music (unlike the girls into R&B or the boys into heavy metal). It was segregation based on taste not race. It was to my disappointment that those two things are more often than not considered conditional to each other, and of all the subcultures I could have picked to identify with I had to pick the whitest: goth.

In 2016, I went to Whitby Goth Festival in the UK, one of the largest gatherings of goth folk in the world, where twice a year throngs of the black-velveted, top-hatted and corseted gather under the skeletal remains of Whitby Abby, and where Count Dracula's ship, heavy with Transylvanian soil and light on rats, first landed in England. I started my trip with my friend Sarah in Manchester, and with the Smiths & Morrissey guidebook in hand I posed for pics in front of the Salford Lad's Club and the gates of "Cemetery Gates." Then we made our way south to Macclesfield. It was a cold and drizzly day and as we stood shivering at Ian Curtis' grave, I was more moved than I expected to be. We stopped briefly at his house on Barton

Street, but it felt a bit ghoulish to be so close to the kitchen where he hanged himself. My other goals on my goth vacation were to: 1. Walk on the Moors, and 2. Stand on cliff, wandering above a sea of fog with Caspar David Friedrich-like contemplation.

I did manage to stand across the road from the Moors and I did stand on the roof of Whitby Pavilion, bracing myself against the wind above the roaring North Sea, while Victorian-ish gentlemen tightly gripped their top hats and women teetered cautiously in fetishy high heels down the stairs. We went to the Abbey where I posed for obligatory pictures among the ruins, and to the Bram Stoker's Dracula Museum (a spooky funhouse dedicated specifically to the 1992 Francis Ford Coppola film) and I bought a broach made of Whitby jet. I had never seen so many goths in one place: whole goth Addams's families, moms and dads with their Baby Bats in tow. As a subculture, goth has tremendous consistency, its affiliates maintaining a spirit of macabre glamor, regardless of age. Once a goth always a goth. From Edward Gorey to Edward Scissorhands, the particulars may morph but the foundation is the same: an anachronistic romanticism, theatrical melancholia, nocturnality, campy morbidity, and the color black.

While the word "gothic" has been applied to literature, art, and architecture since the eighteenth century, "goth" emerged in the late 1970s as the aggression of punk turned inward into the more introspective and cerebral post-punk. The Doors, Alice Cooper, and the Velvet Underground have been described as being "gothic," but goth music and its eponymous subculture truly originated in 1978 with the release of Joy Division's album *Unknown Pleasures*. Ian

Whitby Abbey / Joy Division plaque near Ian Curtis' house,
photos by L. Taylor

Curtis' voice felt unusually deep for someone so young and their music had the dissonant quality of a catchy pop tune with self-deprecating lyrics about personal pain. Peter Saville's brilliant cover, which has become iconic to the point of parody, even feels like a different kind of gothic, a modern gothic, minimalist and scientific. Joy Division is a cooled kind of romanticism, one that is less focused on the haunted and ghostly, but on the everyday of the here and now. It's not the gothic born from a dark and stormy night in a villa in Switzerland, but from an employment service office in Macclesfield.

With the debut of "Bela Lugosi's Dead" in 1979, Bauhaus became the quintessential goth band. Then Siouxsie came along and sang about the ashes of Pompeii, childhood nightmares, and mad arsonists. Her fetishy punk clothes and Cleopatra eyeliner crystallized a dark sensuality, which has sustained to this day. Robert Smith of the Cure broke against gendered codes of masculinity with his untamed spiky mane of hair, red lipstick and sad love songs about boys not crying, and an aesthetic to this dark whimsy was solidified — a synthesis of glam, punk, fetish, Victorianism, Medievalism and assorted macabre accoutrement. The subculture that was born from this music began to materialize into a recognizable style, introducing a visual vocabulary to its maudlin language. In describing goth to others, I like to say, "Imagine a peacock. Now imagine a peacock that's all black." The uninitiated see black and assume anger or sorrow, but they miss the camp. The goth that I know is more dandies and vamps than doom and gloom.

Goth in popular culture evokes images of alienated suburban youths with an aura of self-indulgent angst. In 1988, Winona Ryder brought us the strange and unusual Lydia Deetz in Tim Burton's *Beetlejuice*. In 1997 on *Saturday Night Live*, Chris Kattan introduced the character Azrael Abyss and the "resplendent darkness" of his parent's house in Tampa, Florida. When he isn't hosting his cable access show, "Goth Talk," the Prince of Sorrow works at a Cinnabon at the mall. And perhaps the nail in the coffin, the opening of the one-stop goth shop Hot Topic.

Once the caricature was cemented, goth became ripe for parody, and this seems to mark the start of a fractionating of the subculture into further sub-subcultures. Goth stopped being a consolidated fringe group and became a marketing tool, a sellable product and a label that could be placed on anything that looked the part. Instead of goth being something that you *were*, goth was now something you could buy. In 2000, Angelina Jolie wore a Morticia Addams-style tight long, black dress with long, straight black hair and cat-eye eyeliner to the Oscars and the media immediately labeled her a Goth Queen. Granted she also wore a vial of her then-boyfriend Billy Bob Thornton's blood around her neck, so I should probably give her more cred, but soon all it took was a lacy black gown and a smoky eye to be considered goth. As goth became more commodified and embraced by popular culture, the more it adapted to maintain its otherness. It is precisely the specificity of the display of goth that makes it easy to mimic and easy to mock. In order for goth to remain other, it had to become more complicated.

I should have prefaced all of this by saying that the

goth that I describe is *my* goth, the goth of *my* youth in the Eighties. Since then all sorts of goth sects have emerged, blending genres and merging with other subcultures to form even more specific identities with their own particular accoutrement and markers: Cyber goths, Fetish goths, Rock-a-Billy goths, Victorian goths, Vampire goths, Bubble goths, Hippy goths, Tribal goths, Fairy goths, Cabaret goths, Corporate goths — there was even a paradoxical moment for Health goths... I suppose I would fall into the Traditional goth category or (god forbid) Elder goth.

Goth alone is too big, too broad, encompassing multitudes of fashion and ever-expanding musical styles. The Victorian goths have their mourning drag, the Vampire goths their custom fangs, Rock-a-Billy goths their Bettie Page bangs. Since fashion plays such a vital role, it's easy to dismiss goth purely as style or an affectation. But its ostentatious display is a vital aspect of its dissent. Goth represents a resistance to the mainstream, a self-identifying otherness, a skepticism of blind optimism, with a *memento mori modus operandi*. It is the melodramatic *élan* to the dull hegemonic culture of positivity. Goth isn't just fashion, it is a sensibility and perspective on the world, a *gothic* perspective. Goth style developed from music that came from Britain and with it a European aesthetic, but what if one's perspective isn't British or European, or white for that matter? What does that look like? What are the signs and accoutrements of African American gothness? Is there such a thing as AfroGoth?

Tracey, photo by Fred Berger for Propaganda Magazine, *1984*

In the spring of 1984, when goth was still in its post-punk nascence, Fred Berger, editor-in-chief of *Propaganda* magazine, spotted Tracy while walking in Manhattan's East Village. She told him that her favorite club was

Danceteria, her favorite record store was Bleeker Bob's, and her favorite band was Bauhaus.[2] She's not wearing much makeup, if any, and her pressed hair is spiked up just enough to register as punk. There's no leather or fishnets, no dramatic eye shadow or a surplus of accessories. It's just a black girl in a Bauhaus t-shirt and to me Tracey seemed gothest of them all.

Be Blacker

If I could pinpoint a date when I formally lost any goth affiliation I might have had, I would say it was sometime between 1987 and 1992. 1987 marked the year my family moved from Detroit to Cincinnati, Ohio and in 1992 the Cure released "Friday I'm in Love." In Detroit I saw all kinds of Black kids: kids into hip-hop, nerdy kids into *Star Trek*, rich Black kids, poor Black kids, popular Black kids and arty-farty Black kids like me. When I started at Renaissance High School, I slipped relatively seamlessly into a world of sensitive alternative types — young Socialists, boys dressed in black who smoked and wrote poetry, and Black girls who listened to R.E.M. and everyone seemed to be bi. My Blackness was just one of many and not all that interesting.

When we moved to Cincinnati, I lost my natal clique of weirdos, and if I was just poetically angst-ridden before, Ohio kicked it up (or down) quite a few notches to just boring old depression. Walnut Hills High School was missing the diversity of Blackness that I experienced in

Detroit, and I never met any dark-skinned freaks like me. At lunch the Black kids congregated on the front steps, with brightly colored clothes and perfectly straightened hair (which I never managed to master) and they all seemed to have known each other all their lives. I mostly hid in the art room.

One day, in response to the fall of the Berlin Wall, some students built a wall made of boxes of office paper six-feet high, dividing the main hallway into a makeshift East Walnut and West Walnut. But, this political exercise inadvertently ended up creating a starkly drawn line between where the Black kids hung out and the white kids hung out, evoking more of a Jim Crow vibe than the DDR. And I was on the wrong side of the wall. Again.

I stayed in Ohio through college, and by the time the Nineties came around, my accessories had simplified and I spent most weekends at gay clubs dancing to techno and house music. I wore colors. I was in the Graphic Design program at the University of Cincinnati and plunged myself into the very un-goth world of Swiss minimalism, modernism, and form that followed function.

One day I was approached by two students preparing a seminar on "minorities" in design. Since I was the only Black person in the department they wanted some assurance that I would be there and hoped I would contribute to the discussion. They asked me, completely in earnest, if I would "act as Black as possible." I gaped at them with confusion, but before I could ask them what the fuck was that supposed to mean, they blurted a chipper, "Thanks!" and walked away.

Of course, I knew exactly what they meant. I knew they didn't mean I should act "Oprah Winfrey" Black or "Condoleezza Rice" Black. I knew they didn't even consider "Grace Jones" Black and wouldn't even know about "Poly Styrene" Black. I didn't have a crystal clear vision of the Black person they had in their mind, but I imagine they were thinking something loud and sassy with lots of neck rolling and finger snapping. I wanted to stroll in the next morning, fifteen minutes late with a Colt .45 in one hand and a bucket of fried chicken in the other. Or I could have picked my hair out into an Angela Davis afro and stood defiantly head down and fist up. Maybe I'd recite some def poetry? I resigned myself to a silent protest, refusing to participate.

Out of everything in that encounter, the "as possible" part of that request intrigued me the most. It had inadvertently hit upon something that still haunts Black folks to this day: quantifiable Blackness, Blackness as a scale from "Oreo to ghetto."[3] Challenging me to be "more Black" than I already was, was for them a way to be as "less white" as possible. Perhaps they were worried that I was too much like them and would have a point of view and a frame of reference too close to their own? Apparently, I've never been Black enough to satisfy anyone, Black or white. Ralph Ellison described Blackness as "something-else-ness," a phrase that has an uncanny quality, a weird inconceivability which felt pretty applicable to me.

In an alleyway on a side street near the Gowanus Canal in Brooklyn, one could spend a Friday night drinking cheap red wine and listening to a lecture on spirit photography or the Anatomical Venus or the Grand Guignol. I was drawn to the Morbid Anatomy Museum by an ad for a talk called, "The Saddest Object in the World," given by Evan Michelson, owner of Obscura Antiques & Oddities and goth doyenne of New York City. I became a regular there, but as I looked around the room, like most rooms in most places I went to, I was often the only Black person, or one of two or three at the most. Still.

I started this project with this intent of researching the Black goth scene and what it was like to be a part of a subculture perceived as being "white," how it felt to navigate a world where you are twice marginalized when you are the only one in the room. In a post-Hot Topic, post-Obama world, in a time when Pharrell Williams was making Blerds (Black nerds) cool, was it even an issue? Was there anything really to talk about? Then I found articles online like: "Goth So White? | Black representation in the Post-Punk Scene,"[4] and "Being Weird and Black Doesn't Mean You're Interested in Being White,"[5] and I began to think that not much has changed since that summer at the YWCA. I came across a thread on a message board which began with the statement: *I really hate when I see black goths.*

After several comments mocking photos of Black goth boys and rating the relative hotness of Black goth girls, someone asked, "So's anyone going to explain why black goths are weirder than any other kind of goth?" There was one reply, "Because their black. Seriously, its that simple. [sic]"

There's an acceptance of white weirdness, an assumption that there will always be white folks on the fringes of society with subcultures and affiliations that rebel against conventional norms and societal expectations. But being Black in America is already kind of weird, so despite the mean and racist overtones, that flippant answer was somewhat right. Adding an extra layer of oddity on top of an already marginalized group, flies in the face of "respect-ability politics" and questions the validity of so-called Black authenticity. It's a refusal to conform to social standards despite being taught that conformity to those social norms is the dream, the goal, the endgame, to finally for once *not* be the other. So when normalcy is denied for centuries, the refusal of normalcy is a radical choice. If the illusion of whiteness as the standard of an idealized American persists, Blackness by its nature repudiates that illusion. To then completely reject all notions of stand-ardization is a double condemnation. If lightness is the goal, goth embraces darkness. If white is good, pure, and enlightened, goth chooses black. If gravitas denotes pride, goth embraces whimsey. If Blackness requires vigilance, goth deigns to daydream.

But materially Black goths are pretty much the same as white goths. Goths in Nairobi dress about the same as goths in New Jersey.[6] Goth folks generally like the same stuff, and listen to the same music. These are the things that identify a goth as goth after all. Except that when they go to shows there are fewer of them in the crowd, brown dots in a sea of white. And unlike white goths, they're, well... Black.

In 2003 James Spooner released *Afro-Punk*, a documentary about being Black in the overwhelmingly white punk music scene. The movie spawned a music festival in Brooklyn and has since grown into a global brand encompassing art, journalism, activism, and fashion with festivals in Atlanta, London, Paris, and Johannesburg. Afropunk, the organization, sees itself as "a platform for the alternative and experimental" and "a voice for the unwritten, unwelcome and unheard-of." Today, the phenomena that is Afropunk, is written about extensively and is extremely welcome in fashion magazines and style blogs as photographers flock to the dusty field of Brooklyn's Commodore Barry Park to document a spectrum of Black Birds of Paradise. There is criticism that the festival stopped being about the music, that its corporate sponsorship is antithetical to its purpose, that its focus seems to be more about photo-ops than punk music, that its tenants of radical inclusion have become more lip service than anything. Nonetheless, it remains a space for Black alterity and self-expression, and is a place where an Afrogoth aesthetic fits comfortably with Afrofuturism, Black Dandies, queerness, natural hair and a general Erykah Badu / FKA Twigs vibe.

Midnight Bustle by Kambriel, photo by Nadya Lev, courtesy Kambriel

The proliferation of Afrogoth Facebook groups and Tumblr feeds, provide spaces for goth diaspora visibility in which corsets and vampiric paleness are replaced with African-ish "tribal" jewelry, sculptural braids, beads and patterns of

Theresa Fractale, photo by Marko Smiljanic

white dots on Black faces, proving it is possible to represent gothicness without representing colonialism. Then I came across a photo of a black girl in a shirt that read SO GOTH I WAS BORN BLACK.[7] After the initial "I see what you did there" chuckle, it occurred to me that this was a rather complex concept for a novelty t-shirt. What is the equivalency between "goth-ness" and "Blackness?" What is it about the gothic, beyond the color black, that is Black? Is Blackness inherently gothic?

Most subcultures have a uniform, a style, a language, a posture, something that unifies people together and identifies the "us" versus the "them" — a prescribed and understood visage that signifies I am one of you. But clothes can change, make-up can be removed, poses can drop. One can *feel* goth and not look the part. I like a crisp, white button-down shirt, or a chambray dress now and then. I wear little makeup and prefer a single statement ring rather than one on each finger. Aside from usually wearing black, the only thing that would identify me as a "goth" is if I told you I was. However, what I am immediately and unequivocally seen as is Black. I can't take off my Blackness and change into something else, and if Rachel Dolezal thinks she can do the reverse, she is mistaken.

When I was accused by Black kids of acting white, or when I was asked by my college classmates to act as "Black" as possible, they were critiques of varying constructs of Blackness, neither of which were me. The specificity of the goth aesthetic is clear, Blackness is not. Ellison calls this tension the "blackness of blackness," one unifying theory of Black culture clashing with subjectivity. Blackness is already objectified and marginalized, but with the addition of a qualifier (Black + goth) the otherness is doubled. It pushes the margins off of the page. It's being Blacker than Black and what is more black than goth? If you'll allow me the *This is Spinal Tap* reference, there's none. None more black.

Goth (or punk or any other subculture outside of the mainstream) exists both inside and outside of society. Goth kids wouldn't be weird if there weren't any normal kids to compare them to. Blackness is the same —it wouldn't exist without non-Blackness to compare it to. Both goth and Blackness are performative identities with foundations in transgression, a familiarity with death and aestheticized mourning, and a keen awareness of the darker side of human nature. Poet and scholar Fred Moten wrote that "black performance and black radicalism" are inseparable, that Blackness comes with a built-in resistance to objectification, and that this is "the 'essence' of black performance and indeed the 'essence' of blackness itself." Otherness *is* Blackness. As Sacha Jenkins from the band the 1865 says, "When you're Black you're punk rock all the time."

Gothic

This book is about more than goths. Goth is too specific a term, too loaded with affiliations that aren't my own. The goth-ness of Blackness can't be found in the usual haunts, so for that we must go back to its origins and put back the "ic." The words gothic and goth can mean very different things to different people, but they have attributes that run parallel to each other and occasionally overlap. While they share a similar bone structure, they inhabit slightly different bodies. While both words have different cultural and historical origins, they both conjure the same images of gloom, the macabre, the melancholy, and the romantic. They are both slightly out of place and out of season from the rest of the world and they both take pleasure and comfort in those things that ought to repel and disgust. They both snip off the rose bloom in favor of the thorny stem.

Cologne Cathedral. Cologne, Northrhine-Westfalia, Germany

Poster for a marathon reading of Dante's Inferno, *held annually during Holy Week at the Cathedral of St. John the Divine in New York, Client: The Cathedral Church of St. John the Divine, Designer: Michael Bierut, Firm: Pentagram, Date: 2009*

Goth is a music genre and its associated subculture, but the gothic is much broader in scope. It can represent a fifth-century Barbarian tribe, a seventeenth-century post-Reformation political affiliation, or a medieval revivalist style of architecture. It's a genre of literature that spans from Mary Shelley to Stephen King. It's a category of typefaces, ironically not the medieval blackletter, but modernist sans serifs. St. Patrick's Cathedral and Matthew Gregory Lewis' novel *The Monk* qualify as gothic, but so does fashion designer Alexander McQueen's 2007 Autumn/Winter collection, "In Memory of Elizabeth Howe, Salem, 1692."

The word "gothic" originates from the Visigoths and the Ostrogoth, Germanic tribes who sacked Rome in 410. The age of Enlightenment brought a rebirth of classical Greek and Roman forms of culture in which everything was to be rational, instructional, proportionate and harmonious. Rome became equated with culture and intellect, and since the Goths busted in and ruined it, "gothic" became a pejorative. Gothic became synonymous with the Middle Ages and a belief in the superstitions, the supernatural, the obsolete, and outlandish. Gothic architecture with its spiky, skeletal, overly ornate arches, was considered vulgar and barbaric. Gothic novels and their neo-medieval romanticism were thought to be a bit trashy.

In the mid-eighteenth century, a new form of romantic literature emerged that renounced the rationality of neoclassicism and embraced the phantasmagoric. The dull predictability of scientific reason did not have the same thrill that comes with submission to uncertainty. Horace Walpole's *The Castle of Otranto*, published in 1764, was a throwback to the age of chivalry that centered on old familial curses, doomed romances, and tragic deaths. Complete with dark passageways, trapdoors, mysterious noises, and paintings that move by themselves, it is considered to be the first gothic novel, and would set the tone for a genre spanning from Edgar Allan Poe to *Scooby-Doo*.

Gothic is less of a genre and more of a mode, a way of thinking, more of a sensibility than a style. While England is the birthplace of the gothic, the ingredients that make up the aesthetic allows for a fluidity that opens up a reading not limited to Europe. Gloomy skies, desolate landscapes and decrepit buildings are not the sole domain of the United Kingdom and not the only topographical and meteorological means of establishing gloom. Darkness is everywhere, even in oppressive glare of the noonday sun.

American Gothic

"My name is Fountain Hughes. I was born in Charlottesville, Virginia. My grandfather belonged to Thomas Jefferson." Hermond Norwood recorded his interview with "Uncle Fountain" as he calls him, in Baltimore, Maryland in 1949 as part of the Works Progress Administration (WPA) program. There's a pause after he introduces himself and you can hear the sound of dishes clinking together over the soft hiss of the recording. There's an occasional car horn and squeak of a chair. Hughes lectures him about the dangers of debt and how at the age of one hundred and one he doesn't owe anyone anything. "Don't spend your money before you get it. So many colored people head over heels in debt." Norwood asks him how far back he can remember, and he says, "Things come to me in spells. I remember things more when I'm laying down than when I'm walking around." He begins another train of thought about children's shoes and how he didn't have a pair until he was twelve years old. Norwood asks him who he worked for and he responds, "You mean when I was a slave?" He talks about the slaves on the auction block being bought and sold like cattle, about his master not being too bad. He talks about trying to survive after they were freed, sleeping wherever they could, let loose into the world with no money, no education and no home. His voice is softer, sadder, and while I want to know more, I miss the passion and vigor he had when he was talking about fiscal responsibility. The recording is clear, the voice loud, the fidelity is better than the last conference call I had on my cell phone. While he may be long dead, Fountain Hughes sounds like he's right here, right now, and I'm reminded again that there are only few generations between me and Monticello.

Thomas Jefferson inherited his first thirty slaves from his father (he'd own 607 over his lifetime) — the same year Walpole published *The Castle of Otranto*.[8] In that year, 1764, the rumblings of the Revolution were just beginning, but America and England were still about forty years away from ending the slave trade (it lingered longer in Brazil and Cuba). In 1818, Mary Shelly released her modern Prometheus to the world, John Polidori was about to introduce us to our first gentleman vampire, and Frederick Douglas was born into slavery. The narratives that inform our language of terror were beginning to take shape while the seeds of a home-grown American gothic were starting to take root.

In the discourse about the slave trade there are few words that encapsulate the origins of America better than "horror." According to Ann Radcliffe, the defining attribute of horror is the "unambiguous display of atrocity." She was making a critique of the literary works of her gothic contemporaries, but I can't think of a better way to express the Middle Passage.

Blackness in America is still in the middle, residing in the place between opposites: living in the present while carrying the past, being human but perceived as other, considered both a person and a product, both American and foreign, neither here nor there. Most gothic tales start with a journey: *Frankenstein* is an epistolary tale that begins with a journey at sea, there is something almost bureaucratic about *Dracula* as Harker details the minutia of his business trip abroad, and portions of *The Mysteries of Udolpho* read like a travel blog as the heroine describes the scenic view from her carriage of the hills of Italy. Whether it is crossing the threshold into a haunted house or crossing the Atlantic, all horror stories start with a lacuna, the nothingness of the space between places.

Saidiya Hartman writes that "the most universal definition of the slave is a stranger," and being a stranger in a strange land is a classic way to create a sense of vulnerability, and the fear of the foreign is part of the vocabulary of horror. Early gothic writers often placed their protagonists in Catholic countries where archaic superstitions still thrived, distancing them from their enlightened Anglican England: *The Monk* is set in Spain and *The Mysteries of Udolpho* is in Italy, *Dracula* goes back and forth between Britain and Eastern Europe. It seems like every year there is a new movie about naïve city tourists lost in the woods or the entitled ugly American in a foreign country (*Deliverance, Hostel, The Blair Witch Project*). In these stories characters are taken out of the comfort and control of their environment (usually voluntarily) and inserted into an alien atmosphere with unfamiliar customs, locations and languages. It's a powerlessness that parallels the forced displacement of captive Africans caught in the psychic Bermuda triangle between Africa, the Caribbean, and America. For those who survived, it must have felt like a living purgatory, something in between life and death, here and there, the known and the unknown. Limbo is supposed to be a space of waiting, something in between heaven and hell. But limbo also represents a state of oblivion and nothingness. It's both a transition and a place of imprisonment, a home for the disappeared.

Slavers Throwing overboard the Dead and Dying
— Typhoon coming on, *J. M. W. Turner, 1840*

From The Book of Drexciya, Volume 1, *Haqq & Estevam*

The Middle Passage was a "non-place," a space of dread, not only in between land and languages, but between perceptions of the world and states of being. It was a dislocation from one's history, culture, identity and autonomy, a horrifying liminality between the familiar old and the terrifying new. The journey through the trade route from Europe to Africa to the Americas and West Indies could last anywhere from one to three months, during which hundreds of Africans were packed into the hulls of ships, chained next to people whose language they didn't speak, sitting in their own waste in sweltering heat and stifling air. Some succumbed to dysentery, dehydration, malnutrition, some refused to eat in despair, some threw themselves overboard, risking the chance of a punishing afterlife for the possibility of returning home to their ancestors passed.

At the United Nations headquarters in New York City, a memorial was installed marking the (less than elegantly named) International Day of Remembrance of the Victims of Slavery and the Transatlantic Slave Trade. *The Ark of Return* was designed by Rodney Leon, an American architect of Haitian descent. Part of the memorial, features a figure of a man lying on his back carved from black Zimbabwean granite, wrapped in a shroud of white marble. He's not reclining comfortably, his left arm is stretched out, his neck straining to keep his head raised, a position suggesting that of a slave pressed on to the floor of a ship, barely able to move but still reaching upward. Unlike the still flat figure of the memorialized dead carved into funeral tombs, this figure is either refusing to succumb or is attempting to rise. The intent of the sculpture is "to psychologically and spiritually transport visitors to a place where acknowledgement, education, reflection and healing can take place," but there is something tragic about this figure. He lies in a tomb-like angular structure evocative of a ship, he is reaching up just slightly and his head is lifted, but is frozen solid to the marble. The posture suggests a state of paralysis, trying to wake from a dream but unable to rise. He is not yet dead but trapped in memoriam.

Part of the horror of these deaths along the Middle Passage is the lack of memorialization — these are the unknown, the unnamed, lives that have disappeared under duress and deaths destined for haunting. Theirs are stories we will never hear, people we will never know, lost in the Tomb of the Unknown that is the Atlantic Ocean. When we think of haunted spaces, we think of structures or defined areas with clear borders. Can the sea be haunted? How does a ghost inhabit that which has no borders, something formless that ebbs and flows?

In the four-album compilation *Journey of the Deep Sea Dweller*, the Detroit electronic band, Drexciya, imagined a mythology of an underwater country populated by the unborn children of pregnant African women who were thrown off of slave ships. The babies adapted to breathe underwater in their mothers' wombs and a society is formed of sea-dwelling Black people fathoms below the plantations and the prisons. It is an idealistic notion, a cross between Atlantis and Wakanda and one that takes the retrospective romanticism of the gothic with the addition of a speculative "what if." The offspring of the dead have created a world of their own, and I can imagine the black figure in the *Ark* breaking out of his marble tomb and floating up over the East River, over Queens, dodging airplanes over JFK airport, out across the sea, back home.

Southern Gothic

The gothic is a location as much as it is an atmosphere. The foggy streets of England, the mountains of Romania, the haunted forests of Japan and Germany… every country has its ghosts. When we think of the American Gothic, two things typically come to mind: either the Grant Wood painting of the stoic farmer and his wife or the Southern Gothic.

I'm not Southern. I am a Mid-Westerner raised in the Northeast and my people are from Kansas, Indiana, and Ohio. I'm used to fields of wheat not cotton. I don't carry hot sauce in my bag and when the temperature creeps above seventy-five degrees I start getting cranky. The first time I saw a Confederate Flag waving was out of someone's dorm room window at Yale. Then in 2016, Beyoncé's video "Formation" came out and for one fleeting moment I wished I had grown up in the South and gone to an HBCU (Historically Black College or University). I'm pretty indifferent to her music, but the images of black women with fantastic hair, lounging in a dimly lit parlor in *Daughters of the Dust* white Victorian dresses, lazily fanning themselves in the unairconditioned heat, made me envious. I was never a member of this sorority of Southern Black Sisterhood and I felt left out.

She stands front and center on a plantation porch

twirling a waist-long braid flanked by dandyish men in long, black coats and bow ties. There are vines creeping up the worn, white columns, a candelabra hangs from the ceiling above her head, and a welcoming pitcher of water sits on a tea trolley. She wears a long, black, shoulder-less lacy dress and thick layers of silver necklaces piled up high like a Ndebele choker. On her head is an oversized, wide-brimmed, witchy black hat that completely obscures her eyes, suggesting that she can see us while we can't see her, wielding power like a popstar conjure woman. The aging house with wild vegetation, the all-black clothes with dramatic old-world formality, the big black hat — it's a familiar gothic aesthetic, but through the filter of Black Lives Matter. Visually it is lush with Southern Gothic sensibility, but it comes with a particularly Black perspective on dread and death. The mothers of Trayvon Martin, Michael Brown, and Eric Garner hold up photos of their sons killed by the police and the video ends with a little Black boy in a hoodie, that suspect garment of shady juvenile delinquency. He's dancing in front of a phalanx of white law enforcement officers in riot gear and they hold their hands up in surrender. It cuts to a wall spray painted with the phrase, "STOP SHOOTING US."

Beyoncé's Blackness is different from my Blackness, and I don't subscribe to the romantic notion that the closer one is in geography to the Mason-Dixon Line the more authentic their Blackness, but the history of African Americans seems closer to the surface there. The Deep South is the heart of America's Darkness and is the source for the art and music that is uniquely American. Dr. Regina N. Bradley puts it better:

The first thing I immediately thought when I saw Beyoncé's "Formation" was that some folks ruts – "roots" – would show. You know, ruts: biases, fears of lineage, missing genealogies, shit like that. And folks don't like their ruts or their slip showing. Beyoncé showed er'body's slip, parasol, skeeta bite scars, and conjuring grandmamma essence in this video. And it was scary. Downright gothic. That is, of course, unless you're southern – by affiliation or blood and maybe hot sauce preference – and your ruts are ALWAYS showing because there was no reason to hide them in the first place.

The traditional gothic atmosphere is foggy darkness and English damp, but the Southern Gothic climate is a sweltering humidity and oppressively blinding sun.[9] Instead of tiptoeing through the dark passageways of a decrepit castle on a remote mountain, the Southern Gothic sits in a rocking chair on a wrap-around porch with a paper fan in one hand and a glass of bourbon in the other. Instead of ghosts, vampires, or resurrected corpses, the phantoms that haunt gothic narratives are the ramifications of racism, repressed guilt, social pariahs, and marginalized freaks.

I have a clear picture in my head when I hear the phrase Southern Gothic, and it's of Tennessee Williams' Maggie the Cat in a white slip pining as her gay husband struggles with a crutch in one hand a glass of whiskey in the other. It's the middle-aged, cotton gin-owning Archer Lee, married to a nineteen-year-old virgin who sucks her thumb and sleeps in a crib. Southern Gothic evokes images of old women telling stories of dark underbellies and old family secrets, of Faulkner's "failed dynasties of the old ascendancy… all unwitting builders of haunted houses." The Southern Gothic is a specific kind of American ghost story that evokes the miasma of dusty rural towns and abandoned plantations, troubled misfits and miscreants, haunted by any number of sins and secrets. It is a genre of fiction born out of the emancipated South where the grotesqueries of the human condition are the monsters, and the narrators and storytellers are usually white.

The dread of post-slavery economic decline threatened to shatter the image of the idyllic Dixieland and cast a cloud of disgrace over old traditions and a certain "way of life" that Northerners just wouldn't understand. If the source of the gothic in England is a romanticizing of the past, the Southern Gothic is a deglamorization of the antebellum Dixie. The technicolor sunset over Tara blanches and loses its rhapsodic glow, revealing a darker kind of melodrama.

Closets and Walls

The Danes have *hygge* and the Japanese have *wabi-sabi*: words that express a unique characteristic of that country which cannot easily be translated. Similarly, in America, we have our own particularly American characteristic — a sense of unease, a lingering creepy aura from the darkness of the country's foundation, but as yet it remains unnamed.

There's a reason why American horror movies still use

the old tired trope of haunted houses built on "ancient Indian burial grounds." America is built *over* the bones of brown people who were here first, and built *by* Black people brought here against their will, and the fear of retaliation is real. But more than that, there is the persistent self-delusion that our gains are not ill-gotten, that slavery wasn't *that* bad, that it was so long ago and we should be over it by now.

The gothic is a retrograde form of romanticism, but America is a forward-looking country — a Manifest Destiny projection to some idealized point in the horizon, and we do not like to be reminded of the sordid path we've taken on the way there. I wish there was a word or phrase that named this particularly American anxiety — the unsettled unease of knowing that at any moment the jig may be up. We need a phrase of our own for the muffled heartbeat under the floorboards, the fetid goo oozing from the walls, the screams coming from behind the wall, the festering guilt that comes with getting away with murder. The uncanny occurs when what was supposed to be "secret and hidden but has come to light."[10] What is the word then for the fear of exposure, a phrase that represents a fear of accountability? The colloquialism "skeleton in the closet" is the closest I have come, and it has a telling origin, going back to 1816 in a British journal on hereditary diseases: "… men seem afraid of enquiring after truth; cautions on cautions are multiplied, to conceal the skeleton in the closet or to prevent its escape."

We use it to describe a secret, a hidden fact which if exposed could have damaging repercussions — the dirty truth that stains something perceived as clean and good.

It has an element of horror: a corpse stashed away and left to rot until there's nothing left but bones. Another version of "skeleton in the closet" used in the late nineteenth century was, "a nigger in the woodpile." It was originally meant as a reference to the underground railroad and the practice of hiding fugitive slaves under piles of firewood. The source of America's festering corruption was the slave, the original skeleton.

Horror has always been used to illuminate cultural anxieties and gives a voice to our collective fears. So, what to make of the gothic in America, a place which by the very nature of its founding is predisposed to a culture of anxiety? The dread of knowing the enemy at the gate is understandable, but in America the enemy has already passed through it, and has been brought inside. The call is coming from inside the house.

Through tales of horror and hauntings, by digging into graves and walking into the deep darkness, the gothic metabolizes historic trauma into art. Like historical ectoplasm, the past oozes from orifices in literature, music, film, and art. The gothic aestheticizes the atrocity, giving us a method to process the pain and confront the fear, on our own terms, in our own way. So, what does Black trauma look like? What does it sound like? If, as the t-shirt suggests, "goth-ness" is quantifiable by "Blackness," is the American gothic ontologically Black?[11]

Mural dedicated to Edgar Allan Poe on the Spring Garden Apartments
public housing complex in Philadelphia, Pennsylvania,
photo by Barb Hauck-Mah, via Flickr

The taxi driver stopped at the entrance to the Spring Garden Apartments and I looked back and forth between my phone and the street. I was far away from The Liberty Bell and Independence Hall and all the other standard historic spots in Philadelphia and thought to myself, "I know Poe didn't live in the Projects." I looked at the rows of uniform houses to my left and a large brick house completely covered in scaffolding before realizing that I had the right place. Behind the dense grid of steel frames and blue industrial tarp was indeed the Edgar Allan Poe National Historic Site, Poe's home in Philadelphia, Pennsylvania, from 1837 to 1844.

When I was in the ninth grade my English teacher gave

me an old copy of the works of Poe. It was lost long ago, but I remember accepting the book, with its worn red binding and the yellowed pages, with a little bit of awe. While by no means valuable, its age felt special, something that was passed down, or found, not just bought in a Barnes & Noble. "The Raven" was the first (and only) poem I ever memorized.

If there was a patron saint of the American gothic, it would be Edgar Allan Poe. "The Pit and the Pendulum," "The Tell-Tale Heart," "The Fall of the House of Usher," and of course "The Raven," are standards of the American literary canon as much as Mark Twain or Walt Whitman. His floppy black hair, broad forehead, and sunken eyes have graced t-shirts, posters, tote bags, coffee mugs, and greeting cards, and I myself have a Poe action figure on my desk. In the episode "Dawn of the Posers" on *South Park,* the goth kids create an unlikely alliance with the Vampire kids against the growing proliferation of emos. In an ultimate act of desperation, they summon the ghost of Edgar Allan Poe for help. Poe's apparition floats above the goths, emos and vampires, takes a drag from a cigarette and declares all of them "posers."

Poe was a white man born in 1809, so like most figures and "heroes" from American history, he is problematic. He was both northern and southern — born in Boston, raised in Virginia — he lived, worked, and died in New York, Philadelphia, and Maryland. But one's affiliation with either the north or the south doesn't automatically exonerate one or condemn the other. We know his family owned at least one slave, because he sold one on their behalf.

In his only novel, *The Narrative of Arthur Gordon Pym of Nantucket*, Black and Native American characters are described as ferocious bloodthirsty savages. His stories like, "The Black Cat" and "Gold Bug," have been read as metaphors for the fear of slave insurgencies and he consistently extols the color white to imply purity and black as monstrous. Then there's that cocky, big black bird. He doesn't have H.P. Lovecraft's blatant xenophobia, but a more liquid unease wrought with guilt which seems more appropriate for American horror. Poe's anxiety is a particularly American one, wary of this sleeping giant and its ramifications. Toni Morrison writes that romance (or the gothic) expresses:

> Americans' fear of being outcast, of failings of powerlessness; their fear of boundarylessness, of Nature unbridled and crouched for attack; their fear of the absence of so-called civilization; their fear of loneliness, of aggression both external and internal. In short, the terror of human freedom-the thing they coveted most of all. [Romance] offered platforms for moralizing and fabulation, and for the imaginative entertainment of violence, sublime incredibility, and terror-and terror's most significant, overweening ingredient: darkness, with all the connotative value it awakened.

"The Tell-Tale Heart," "The Black Cat," and "The Fall of the House of Usher," all have a similar theme: the attempt to get away with murder and the effort to deny it. Guilt haunts these protagonists, drives them mad, and that madness leads to their downfall. The black cat that was brought into the home and domesticated becomes the focus of wrath:

> I slipped a noose about its neck and hung it to the limb of a tree, — hung it with the tears of remorse at my heart; — hung it *because* I knew that it had loved me, and *because* I felt it had given me no reason of offense; — hung it *because* I knew that in doing I was committing a sin.

Walls were Poe's go-to place for hiding corpses. He keeps the bodies close, he keeps them in the structure of the home, in the place where we think we are the most safe and secure, but where the evidence is right on the other side of the plaster, just inches away from the head of the bed. His protagonists live with their victims, stash them away, and try to go about their daily lives in an attempt to forget what they have done. He "soundly and tranquilly slept; aye *slept* even with the burden upon my soul." In both "The Tell-Tale Heart" and "The Black Cat," the killers are confident with the police, allowing them into their home with the self-assured presumption of camaraderie with the authorities, that only the privileged can afford. But they are tormented by their guilt, by "the beating of the hideous heart" and the "wailing shriek, half of horror and half of triumph." In Poe's America, they don't get away with it.

BASED ON A TRUE STORY

The proper subject for American Gothic is the black man, from whose shadow we have not yet emerged, that ours is a literature of darkness and the grotesque in a land of light and affirmation.
— Leslie A. Fiedler, *Love and Death in the American Novel*

The past is never dead. It's not even past.
— William Faulkner, *Requiem for a Nun*

This is a true story. Late one night when I was ten or eleven, I lay in bed, not yet asleep, and saw a large black dog walk across my room and out of my bedroom door. We didn't own a dog. I immediately got up and walked through the bathroom to my parents' bedroom and glanced down to find what looked like a white German Shepherd curled up in the bathtub. I shook my dad awake whispering, "Dad, there are dogs in the house!" He drowsily got up to search, but there were no signs of any canine invaders. He assured me that I was only dreaming, but I went back to bed knowing that I saw what I saw. A few days later my mom would confide in me that one night she had woken up from a deep sleep and saw a group of little lap dogs — Chihuahuas, Yorkshire terriers and Pomeranians — hovering in a circle above her head. I knew that there had been a fire in the house long before we moved in, and I was convinced that it had previously been an animal shelter or a vet and now we were haunted by the ghosts of dogs who had succumbed in the flames.

Mine was a Disney-free childhood — my parents didn't want me indoctrinated with any of that Prince Charming / Sleeping Beauty crap, and at the time there were no Black princesses. The first thing I remember learning about Walt Disney was that "he was a fascist." But that kind of fantasy never interested me anyway. I was far more fascinated in the doubtful fantasy, the near-real: life-after-death, ghosts, hauntings, astral projection, psychic powers, anything that was in the *Time-Life: Mysteries of the Unknown* book series.

I never believed in Santa Claus, I was told that he was a spirit of goodness and giving and fun and all of those things, but a bearded fat man in a red suit was not going to come down my chimney. It didn't matter if I knew the truth, I still put cookies and milk out and I still went to bed in delirious anticipation, listening for distant sleigh-bells. Knowing the truth never ruined Christmas for me, because I allowed myself to believe. I decided for myself that for that night (and that night only), Santa was real.

Horror is the one fictional genre that routinely asks its readers to believe them. The archetypal haunted house story, *The Castle of Otranto*, was published anonymously in 1764 with a preface claiming that the book was discovered in 1592 but was believed to have been written between 1095 and 1243. The specifics of the dates and the admission of uncertain origin give an air of plausibility. The possibility that this was a real account with documentary proof added to the allure, but it wasn't until the novel became a bestseller that the writer — Gothic revivalist, parliamentarian, and son of England's first prime minister, Horace Walpole[1] — took credit for making it all up. In the second edition, Walpole added a subtitle, *The Castle of Otranto: A Gothic Story*, and a horror formula was born.

Similarly, Tobe Hooper's 1974 classic begins with this preface:

> The film which you are about to see is an account of the tragedy which befell a group of five youths [...] The events of that day were to lead to the discovery of one of the most bizarre crimes in the annals of American history, The Texas Chain Saw Massacre.

We know now that this is a ploy to drum up buzz and amp up the fear (it was implemented to perfection in *The Blair Witch Project*), but it always begs the question that something of it must be real. The very real Ed Gein, who used human skulls as bedposts and made belts out of women's nipples, was the inspiration for the chainsaw-brandishing Leather Face, not to mention Norman Bates and Hannibal Lecter. *The Exorcist* and *The Amityville Horror* were gleaned from sort-of real-ish events. Don't all legends start with a grain of truth? We delight in the tiny thrill that comes from that small suspension of disbelief, that inkling that maybe, just maybe, ghosts and monsters do exist, that there is something in the world beyond our power and understanding and that we aren't as safe as we thought we were.

Most people can agree that zombies and vampires don't exist, but when asked, "Do you believe in ghosts?" how many of us say that we do? There are dozens of "reality" ghost-hunting television shows where a troop of intrepid paranormal investigators walk the halls of famous haunted buildings with night vision glasses and EVP recorders jumping at every odd noise and floating orb. The search for proof of life after death goes back centuries; we've tried to measure the weight of souls, captured faint images of loved ones in photographs, and talked to the dead on telephones. Ghosts and haunted houses are the one fictive horror subject that is given the benefit of the doubt. A ghost, after all, used to be a person. It's not an unfathomable creature from another planet, but evidence of the immortal soul, and in this way they are also hopeful. The malevolent ghost, unable to cross over because of some trauma or horrible deed, suggests that what we do while we're alive affects what happens to us when we die, and that we can't escape our history. But if the point of the sublime is to evoke a "twinge of terror" tampered by the security of safety, what then happens when that safety is in doubt, when security is gone?

Beloved

There were times when reading *Beloved* that I dreaded turning the page. Toni Morrison's novel is a cross between a slave narrative and a classic haunted house story, and out of all the ghost stories I've read, it is by far the saddest and the most disturbing. Its supernatural phenomena feel too plausible, inevitable even, and it's heartbreaking to think that the ghosts of slaves could be still tethered to the spot of their pain and demise.

Beloved is the story of Sethe, a runaway slave living in Ohio with her daughter Denver. Their house is haunted by the vengeful spirit of a baby, buried with a headstone marked with the single word, "Beloved," since her mother couldn't afford the extra letters to finish the sentiment "Dearly Beloved." The house emanates an eerie aura, and, although "It's not evil, just sad," the baby ghost is also an angry poltergeist:

> Full of a baby's venom. [...] merely looking in a mirror shattered it [...] two tiny hand prints appeared in the cake [...] another kettleful of chickpeas in a heap on the floor; soda crackers crumbled and strewn in a line next to the door-sill.

Sethe had escaped a life of unfathomable violence at the plantation, ironically named Sweet Home. But after only a month of freedom in Ohio, she was found by slave hunters. Rather than be forced back into captivity and her child sold into slavery, in a state of hopeless panic she slit the throat of her baby daughter. Sethe says, "If I hadn't killed her she would have died and that is something I could not bear to happen to her."

Then one day, eighteen years later, a woman walks out of the river and finds her way to the house at 124 Bluestone Road. The ghost of the baby Beloved has risen from her grave as an young woman with a scar on her throat, singing her mother's lullaby. Sethe devotes herself to taking care of the child, now a woman, she killed. But Beloved sucks the life out of her mother with all the greedy needs of an infant, an infant with a grudge. Despite her mother's attempt to explain to Beloved that she had intended to kill herself and all of her children that day, that they were all supposed to go together, Beloved is unforgiving of her mother for leaving her in her grave all alone:

> Beloved wasn't interested. She said when she cried there was no one. That dead men lay on top of her. That she had nothing to eat. Ghosts without skin stuck their fingers in her and said beloved in the dark and bitch in the light.

The zombie Beloved demands to be seen, acknowledged, fed, and tended to. With the whiplash speed of a child, she goes from wide-eyed singular adoration of her mother, to violent tantrums, and her need for her mother's love and attention is relentless and terrifying. Isolated from the community, abandoned by her lover, and fired from her job, Sethe spends all of her money on fancy food, ribbons and buttons for her daughters, and shrinks into starvation and madness.

Beloved is inspired by the true story of Margaret Garner, who in January 1856 escaped with her family from a plantation in Kentucky to Cincinnati, Ohio. She was found by slave catchers, and under the Fugitive Slave Act, faced the prospect of being taken back to Kentucky and enslaved once again. Before they could take her away, she slit the throat of her two-year-old daughter and attempted to kill her other children to spare them all from a life in bondage. The following occurred when they took her into custody:

Margaret Garner sat as though stupefied, but she roused herself when a compliment was paid her on her fine looking little boy. She replied sadly, "You should have seen my little girl that died, that was the bird." She had a scar on the left side of her forehead running down to her cheekbone. When she was asked how she had come by this mark, she replied only, "White man struck me."[2]

Regarding the film adaptation of *Beloved*, Mark Fisher wrote, "Some viewers complain that *Beloved* should have been reclassified as Horror… well, so should American history." As horrifying as it is, Margaret and Sethe's desperate act is understandable. Her daughter would have spent her life in bondage, worked relentlessly, raped, beaten and dehumanized. Her life would never be her own; her body would never be her own. After the horror that Margaret had been through, when her hard-fought freedom seemed for nothing, death must have seemed like mercy and murder the only recourse.

Candyman

There is no established literary genre of Northeast or Midwest Gothic, but there could be. Every county has its own macabre *genius loci*, every city its seedy under-belly. When I lived in Ohio, conspiracy theorists believed that the logo for the consumer goods company, Proctor & Gamble (one of Cincinnati's largest employers), contained Satanic symbology in its design and there were rumors that one neighborhood had a disproportionately large number of people in the witness protection program. Every place has the potential for horror.

The movie that most closely resembled the place where I grew up, Detroit, was Bernard Rose's *Candyman* (1992), the story of a graduate student researching the urban legend of a murderous boogey-man in the Cabrini–Green housing projects in Chicago. Unlike the suburban sprawl in *Poltergeist* or the quaint town of Amityville, the Candyman lurked in the graffiti-covered, dank hallways of high-rise public housing. Instead of the winding, dark secret tunnels in medieval dungeons or the creaking floorboards of a decrepit Victorian house, the architecture of dread in *Candyman* is that of urban neglect: the lights burnt out in a dismal hallway, the incessant drip, drip, drip of a leaky pipe, or a broken elevator with no way down from the twentieth floor but an isolated stairway.

The legend goes that Daniel Robitaille, born the son of a slave, grew up to be an artist. His talent allowed him into polite society, where he fell in love with a white woman and got her pregnant. But when her father found out he set a lynch mob out to get him. They cut off his hand with a rusty saw, and smeared his body in honey, after which he was stung to death by a swarm of bees. A century later, the Cabrini-Green project would be built on the site where they burned his body, and if you say "Candyman" five times in the mirror, he will crawl out of your bathroom cabinet and gut you with his hook.

Candyman is influenced by true events. In the 1980s, the Grace Abbott Homes were one of the most violent projects in Chicago, with one to three murders occurring a week. On April 22, 1987, fifty-two-year-old Ruth Mae McCoy made a call to 911:

McCoy: Yeah, they throwed the cabinet down.
Dispatcher: From where?
McCoy: I'm in the projects, I'm on the other side. You can reach — can reach my bathroom, they want to come through the bathroom.
Dispatcher: All right ma'am, at what address?
McCoy: 1440 W. 13th St.—apartment 1109. The elevator's working.[3]

Due to an anomaly in the design of the building, some of the apartments in Grace Abbott Homes were connected to each other through a pipe chase, a space in the wall that provided easy access to plumbing fixtures for maintenance. It also provided easy access for thieves. Since the bathroom cabinets were accessible from the other side, all someone had to do was take the cabinet out and crawl through. The police arrived, but when no one answered the door and attempts to get the key from the superintendent failed, they gave up and left. A concerned friend called the next day and the police came again, but wary of a lawsuit, the building's security guards would not let them break down the door. The day after her friend insisted that the building drill McCoy's lock, and when they finally entered, three days after her call to the police, she was found dead from four gunshot wounds.

There are multiple layers of horror within this story, only one of which is the terrifying prospect of an intruder crawling through your bathroom cabinet. There is the reluctance of the employees to act out of fear of reprisal from the management, and the lazy indifference of the police officers amounting to a despicable devaluing of the life of this poor, Black woman. The least amount of effort possible was made to help her, and if it was not for the persistence of her friend it might have been weeks before she was found. But what disturbs me the most is the 911 call in which she felt the need to specify that the elevator was working. She must have known that perhaps saving her life might not be worth the effort if it involved climbing eleven flights of stairs. The moral of her story is, if the Candyman won't get you, poverty, systemic racism, indifferent law enforcement, and underfunded public services will.

Tzvetan Todorov says that the fantastic "occupies the duration of uncertainty," between experiencing something we can't explain and the explanation. Ghost stories and horror movies balance on the edge of the possible the impossible. The houses are familiar, the landscapes are recognizable, the families are typical. One of the most terrifying aspects of films like *Poltergeist* or *The Exorcist* is how normal everything is. We need that connection with ourselves for the fear to take hold. We need, if only for a moment, to believe what is happening to them could happen to us. If we take away the supernatural, strip away the embellishment of urban legends and baby ghosts, the stories of Ruth Mae McCoy and Margaret Garner are certain and explainable. And it could happen to any of us.

Grace Abbott Homes have since been demolished, and I wonder if Ruth Mae McCoy haunts the hallways of whatever is there now. I think I believe in ghosts, or perhaps I want to believe in ghosts. I don't believe in god, I don't think that there is a predesigned order to our lives, and I don't believe in heaven or hell. I've always hated the term agnostic, but it's the closest to what I know, which is that there is a lot we don't know. I don't trust the absolutism of either faith or atheism. Ghosts to me provide the potential for something... else — that what we see isn't the only thing here.

One of my favorite explanations for the existence of ghosts is the trace. Some events are so powerful in their violence or anger that it leaves behind a remnant of that death, like the debossed imprint left through the pages when you press too hard with the pen. The ghost hasn't come back to visit us in the present, rather we are seeing a glimpse of past. I like to think that instead of the spirit invading our space, we have temporarily gained access to theirs. Like the shadows of Hiroshima, it takes an atomic level of anger and pain and fear to leave behind such substantial vestiges, something powerful enough to leave a handprint in a cake, to crawl through the bathroom cabinet.

AMERICAN MONSTER

because white men can't
police their imagination
black people are dying
— Claudia Rankine, *Citizen: An American Lyric*

Being an Other in America, teaches you to imagine what can't
imagine you.
— Margo Jefferson, *Negroland*

In the "Juneteenth" episode of the television show *Atlanta*, Earn and his girlfriend Vanessa go to a fancy Juneteeth party at her friend Monique's mansion. June 19, 1865 marks the date slavery officially ended in Texas, a full two and a half years after the signing of the Emancipation Proclamation. It has become a holiday of sorts to celebrate being free at last. Monique's husband Craig is white and an avid collector of all things Black, including his wife. His office is decorated with photographs of Black luminaries, African sculptures and his own Malcolm X-inspired fan art. Craig offers Earn a Hennessy to replace his Forty Acres, and a Moscow Mule cocktail and asks him if he's ever been to Africa. He's appalled when Earn answers in the negative:

> *Craig:* You gotta go! Man, it's your motherland! Where are your ancestors from? Congo? Ivory Coast? Southeastern Bantu region?

Earn: I don't know, this spooky thing called "slavery"
happened, and my entire ethnic identity was erased, so...

There is a lot I like about this glimpse into the bougie Black
upper-class; a Black woman using her white husband for
his money, the husband using his wife for her Blackness,
Craig's cringe-worthy confidence in his understanding of
Black culture and his financially privileged suggestion that
Earn just "go" to Africa. But what I like most about this
scene is Donald Glover's use of the word "spooky." Spooky
implies an eerie, ghostly feeling, something weird and
undefined. Spooky is an ethereal unease that is difficult
to place, an unformed and obscured aura of something
that is not quite right. The answer to the question, "Where
are your people from?" is complicated, and spooky is a
complicated word.

The word "spook" comes from the Dutch *"spooc,"*
meaning "ghost" or "apparition". In the 1940s spook
became a word for a spy — a clandestine, sneaky person
whose life is in the shadows. About the same time spook
also became a derogatory word for Black people. The
Tuskegee Airmen, the group of Black Air Force fighter
pilots and bombers during World War II, were even
referred to disparagingly as the Spookwaffe. The word
evokes images of the bug-eyed coon, a childlike, cowardly
simpleton prone to superstition. The word carries either
a cartoonish innocence or bitingly racist connotations,
and Earn's snarky use of it is fitting. Dehumanization is
a creepy endeavor. While slavery existed in Africa before
European intervention, the trade in the Americas required
an ideological shift in the perceptions of humanity, an

entirely different classification of being deeper than punitive or economic reasoning. We tend to stop at the sheer horror of it and breeze past the elaborate work it took to make the phantasm of race a reality and the illusions that required its upkeep.

The Three-Fifth Compromise was spooky. In order to ensure that southern states had more seats in the House of Representatives, it was proposed in 1787 that the total number of slaves in a state would be considered three-fifths the total number of white people. Five white people equaled three Black people. The bland mathematical rational of it creates an equation of metaphysical fuzzy math that is creepier the more you consider it. Did those extra two Black people never exist? Are they phantom people who are almost there but not quite? Or can you take two-fifths of a person away from them and if so where would you lose it? An arm and a leg? Could you slice bits away starting from the feet up? Perhaps you could remove something more indicative of humanity instead of body parts. Could you take away a sense of smell and long-term memory? Maybe speech and the ability to draw? The formula requires not only the ability to see a person as a non-person (or rather to not see people at all, but as a population), but to *un-see*. Economic and politically strategic contortions aside, it suggests a creepy theoretical disappearing of people and a willingness to psychically evaporate the body that cleans your floor, cooks your food, works your fields, and bares your children. Like Ellison's invisible man, the three-fifths man walks here among us, yet not all here, not all whole.

I've never celebrated Juneteenth. Like Guy Fawkes Day, it seems to me like an opportunity to represent a kind of enlightened signaling that is less about celebrating what the holiday means, and more about showing that you know the holiday exists. It doesn't mean much to me because Juneteenth celebrates the end of something that didn't really end (or more accurately, it's celebrating something we almost had). If emancipation hadn't slid so easily into share-cropping, if the gains of Reconstruction weren't so quickly lost, if reparations had been issued and official apologies from the Nation given at the time, perhaps I'd want to party with a Frozen Freedom Margarita or a Plantation Master Poison. But to me, it's a hollow holiday celebrating some numinous void that emancipation was supposed to fill, but never did. It's a day of absence. Even more so, there is the lingering unease that it's not quite over, that slavery didn't end, but just keeps shape shifting. It is a weird and creepy fog that has yet to lift.

Gothic narratives were (and still are) a means of working through the discomfort of a changing world through the safety of fiction: fears of industrialization, the speed of scientific discovery, the uncertainty of secularism, epidemics and disease, immigrants and cultural others, nuclear annihilation, climate change... every real social fear has its metaphorical monster. The Kantian negative pleasure of these stories allows us to face these fears, to feel the shudder safe in the knowledge that it will all be over in ninety minutes or so.

Blackness in America has not only never been comfortable, but is a constant source of discomfort.

Blackness is often used as a metaphor for any number of social ills: poverty, crime, violence, drug use, promiscuity, broken families, ignorance... to be Black is to *be* the fear, to be the thing that goes bump in the night hiding under the bed. It is one thing to use literature and film to process social anxieties, but what do you do when *you* are the social anxiety? What do you do when the villagers with torches and pitchforks are coming after you?

Reasonable Dogs

I went to a small hippie preschool in Amherst where my mother was working on her PhD at the University of Massachusetts. Chinua Achebe lived next door. Nikki Giovanni was a friend of the family. The Cosby's kids (the real ones) went to the same school as my brother and sister. It seemed like if you were brainy and Black in the Seventies, Amherst was the place to be. One day at school I was playing outside when I saw someone in the distance with a large black dog. A little white girl standing next to me said that I shouldn't go near it because "the dog didn't like Black people" and would attack me if I got too close. She said this with a snide superiority — not as a warning for my safety, but as proof of my inherent corruption, a threat so palpable that even animals could sense it. I was about five or six at the time, and got my first taste of that unique blend of shame, anger, and fear that comes with disenfranchisement. I believed her enough to be wary of dogs for years after, unsure which ones were cool and which ones were racist. It took me a while to realize that

I had no reason to be afraid of the dog, because that little girl, her parents, the owner of the racist dog — they were afraid of me.

America is unreasonably comfortable with being afraid, to the point of doomsday prepping, gun-clinging pride. The use of fear as a political tactic has been a consistent part of the American story from *The Birth of a Nation* to President Donald Trump's absurd vision of a wall between us and Mexico. The strategic use of the fear of Black and brown people infiltrating and contaminating whiteness, cleverly positions the oppressor as being the oppressed, the violator as the victim. It's quite a trick. The use of terror as a technology of repression is one wrought with contradictions because it requires the powerful to seem weak. What would those at the top of the food chain have to tremble about? The non-person: the wild animal, the creature, the monster, the mysterious other.

I have mixed feelings about the term "other" as the generic empty box at the bottom of that list. It's a boring word for something that is usually anything but boring. But, on the other hand, "other" doesn't try to define what it doesn't understand, and I respect that. White supremacy is reliant on Blackness as unknowable, unfathomable, and strange. If America had a national monster, a symbol like baseball or the bald eagle, it would not be a creature with scales or fur or fangs, but a substance that grows and morphs, expands and retracts, spreads and retreats, like The Blob. Or better yet, something parasitic that mimics whatever happens to be next to it like The Thing. America's boogeyman changes depending on the latest threat, be they Black or Muslim or Latino or gay or trans. Be it feminism or democratic socialism. Our American Blob can shape-shift at a moment's notice.

In a 2006 skit from the *Chappelle's Show* entitled, "The Monsters" (a spoof of 1960s TV show *The Munsters*), a Black werewolf (Dave Chappelle), a Black mummy (Donnell Rawlings), and a Black Frankenstein's monster (Charlie Murphy) live together in a suburban home. The Black Frankenstein's monster goes to work in a corporate office, eagerly anticipating a promotion, but instead his boss warns him that the other employees have complained about his violent bursts of anger. With a classic creature-feature roar he raises his fists in the air in fury then punches a hole straight through his boss's desk. He confronts his mostly white co-workers (while waving an arm he ripped off a colleague) and proclaims:

> Listen up! You racist backstabbers. Ya'll know I'm the hardest worker in the division. I'm tired of tip-toeing around this office so you racists can be comfortable. You scared of Black people? That's your problem. My color shouldn't even be an issue. When you look at me all you should see is a man. Not a Black man.

While the white workers cower in fear, a Black woman shuts down his speech with a smirk and says, "Nigga, you a Frankenstein." He can be as righteous as he can be but he's still a monster. The title of this episode of "The Monsters" is "The System Was Not Designed for Us."

There is a difference between terror and horror, and it's one of the brain and the body. Devendra Varma describes it as the "awful apprehension and sickening realization: between the smell of death and stumbling against a corpse." Terror is the dread of the unknown, the anticipation, the mind filling in the gaps of what isn't there. Terror "leaves something for the imagination to exaggerate."[1] Terror is spooky, horror is gross. *The Texas Chain Saw Massacre* gained the reputation of being one of the goriest horror movies ever made, but there is almost no actual violence shown. We never see someone get massacred with a chainsaw. Terror is the fear of what we think could happen, not what is really happening, and we project our own personal nightmares onto the screen regardless of what may or may not be right in front of us. Terror is pure affect and needs no evidence.

Tactical Fear

"Objective reasonableness" is an ominously banal statement, a phrase that suggests actions based on logic and proof, a cool and clinical justification for irrational and excessive violence. When a law enforcement officer engages in an act of excessive force, the rules of objective reasonableness state that when faced with a similar situation, a reasonable person would act the same way.[2] It is an excuse which creates solidarity among brethren against the chosen other. The law of objective reasonableness depends on a universal understanding and acceptance that non-Black people are reasonable and Black people are scary.

In November 2014, an unidentified man called 911, reporting that a Black man was brandishing a gun in a park in Cleveland, Ohio. The caller said, "The guy keeps pulling it out of his pants. It's probably fake, but you know what, it's scaring the shit out of me." In the video, the Black man is by himself, walking around near a gazebo. He appears to be ambling about, in his own thoughts, twirling the gun around and pulling it in and out of his pants like a six-shooting cowboy in a Western. Police arrived at the scene, pulled up next to him, and within seconds they shot him twice in the chest. He died the next day. The "scary man" was twelve-year-old Tamir Rice. The caller was right — it was a toy gun.

In reporting the incident, Officer Timothy Loehmann describes Tamir as being about twenty. I've seen his picture, and if there was ever an image of baby-faced-ness it would be Tamir. In the video he doesn't look wild or menacing, he just looks bored. The reason Loehmann gave for his reaction was that he was "afraid for his life," a slogan that has tripped off the tongue of those pointing smoking guns at Black backs for hundreds of years as an almost unquestionable legal defense. Even if Tamir's gun was real, the option of de-escalation becomes moot — supposedly, the terror is so great, the threat so eminent, that logic and reason disappear and the instinct to react in defense surpasses the one thing that could have saved Tamir's life: objectivity.

Earlier that year, in August in Ferguson, Missouri, Officer Darren Wilson shot unarmed eighteen-year-old Michael Brown six times, supposedly in self-defense. In his testimony, he too said that he "feared for his life," and described Brown as being like a "demon," and that attempting to restrain him "felt like a five-year-old holding onto Hulk Hogan." Brown is framed as being not simply strong, but preternaturally strong, his Blackness giving him superhuman powers with the demonic strength of the possessed. Wilson testified that he had thought about using his mace or taser but could not reach them in time. He doesn't say in time for what.[3]

How can you prove a reasonable amount of fear? What is the evidentiary proof? The implicit bias against Blackness is bred from hundreds of years of dogma pathologizing the "scary Black man" — men that are genetically predisposed to not only be Mandingo strong, but prone to rage, violence and an inability to temper their emotions. We're conditioned to believe that a Black man is automatically a threat that needs to be taken down as swiftly as possible.

The tactical use of fear has entwined American law enforcement with white supremacy since slavery. Blacks were dangerous creatures — useful when tamed, but violent in the wild and capable of turning on their masters at any moment. The precursor to the police were the Night Rider patrols, an organized system of surveillance and control established to monitor slave activity in an attempt to quash insurrections and escape attempts. Despite what we've been led to believe, there were more slave rebellions than we might have thought — about two hundred alone before the Civil War. When faced with constant psychological torture with no end in sight, physical violence and death were not a good enough deterrent for rebellion. Like Margaret Garner knew, sometimes dead is better. Since the fear of corporeal suffering wasn't enough, metaphysical terrorism might work.

Masters and overseers couldn't be in more than one place at a time, but a ghost could be anywhere, always, an omnipotent spy unseen and unlimited by space and time.[4] Slave owners spread rumors of witches, ghosts, and haunted places, encouraging superstitions and exploiting beliefs in the supernatural. Slaves, already in a state of anxiety and suspicion, were confronted by "ghosts" on horseback, the origins of the Ku Klux Klan's white hooded robes. I don't think Black folks really believed these were supernatural spirits on horseback, but in an environment of constant anxiety, this must have been a particularly bizarre mind-fuck.

The goal of terrorism is to force submission through fear, and the modern police force is a cousin of America's original terrorist organization, the KKK. Law enforcement still uses fear as a method of control, but the reality of who is terrorizing whom gets blurry, especially when civilians join in. Racial profiling is no longer just a tool for those in uniform. Wielding power through fear seems paradoxical, but the ability to use 911 as a weapon is a privilege only non-Black and non-brown people seem to enjoy.

In April 2018, Jennifer Schulte (aka BBQ Becky) called the police on a group of Black people barbecuing in a park in Oakland, California. After harassing the picnickers for using charcoal briquettes in their grill, Schulte told the dispatch officer, "I'm really scared! You gotta come quick!" That same year Holly Hilton, the manager at a Starbucks in Philadelphia, Pennsylvania called the police on two Black men waiting in the store for their friend to arrive. At Yale University, Sarah Braasch called the cops on a Black student working on her master's degree in African Studies for napping in a common room while studying.

"Driving while Black," a reference to the disproportionate number of Black drivers that are pulled over by police, has expanded to: Walking while Black, Standing while Black, Shopping while Black, BBQing while Black, Banking while Black, Napping while Black, Babysitting while Black... merely existing in public becomes a misdemeanor. While these instances may seem ridiculous, it's just the latest in a long trajectory of state-sanctioned xenophobia combined with entitled bravado. It is the holier-than-thou pretense of concern for public safety that bothers me the most. It comes with the smug superiority of the tattle-tale, the confidence that comes from knowing that the law is on their side. But the fear of Blackness is an irrational one, and irrational fear plus power is dangerous.

Donisha Prendergast (granddaughter of Bob Marley) was checking out of an Airbnb with her friends when a white neighbor called the cops. She assumed they were robbing the house because Donisha didn't wave back when she waved at them. I've never been stopped by the police. No one has ever pointed a gun at me and told me to put my hands up, but every time I read another article, watch another video, follow another Twitter thread, my heart rate goes up a little. I've stayed at Airbnbs in predominantly white neighborhoods, I've waited for a friend to show up before ordering a latte in a Starbucks, I've accidently nodded off in a public space while studying in college. I don't know what it feels like to be told to get on the ground, but I do know what it feels like to hope to God I'm not scaring any white people.

Wave Hill is a beautiful public garden in the Bronx overlooking the Hudson River. I'd never been there before and took an unnecessarily annoying route involving a walk through the residential streets of Riverdale, one of the wealthiest neighborhoods in New York City. It has a mostly white population and one of the lowest crime rates in the city. I was alone and unsure of how long it would take me to get to the garden, and as I walked past the large houses I picked up my pace thinking, "I need to get out of here before someone calls the cops on me." I have a prestigious job in a creative field, I dress like a Puritan and I have two master's degrees. None of that mattered. If Henry Louis Gates Jr can get arrested for breaking into his own house, what chance do I have?

In America, twenty-three states have "stand your ground" laws. The law, brought to the forefront by the murder of Trayvon Martin in 2012, states that a person has the right to defend themselves or others against threats, or *perceived* threats, to the point of lethal force regardless of whether safely retreating from the situation might have been possible. *Perceived* is the key word here. How can one prove or disprove a perception? How can you prove if you are scared or not? I have yet to see a case of a Black person "standing their ground." You never hear reports of a Black person shooting a non-Black person out of fear for their life — and it begs the question of who is allowed to be reasonably afraid of whom. The fear of

Blackness is so embedded in the fabric of the country, but it's a fear founded on an imagined threat, hundreds of years of mythology that has never been debunked, and this dialectic between the terrorist and the terrified feeds upon itself. To quote Sara Ahmed:

[Fear] brings them together and moves them apart through the shudders that are felt on the skin, on the surface that surfaces through the encounter. The shivering of the black body is misread as a form of rage, and only then as the "ground" of white fear. In other words, the other is only felt to be fearsome through a misreading, a misreading that is returned by the other through its response of fear...

Jordan Peele's 2017 horror movie *Get Out* opens with a specific kind of dread, one that is familiar both in the world of horror and in the real world of Black lives. A young Black man is walking alone at night on an empty residential street talking to someone on his phone, lost in this "creepy, confusing ass suburb." A car slowly begins to follow him, and he immediately hunches his shoulders and lowers his head in a submissive posture. "OK," he tells himself under his breath. "Just keep walking. Don't do anything stupid. Not today, not me." His manner isn't so much that of fear, but of frustration, the exhaustion of someone tired of this shit. He anticipates harassment and even violence, as do we, the audience. Before Eric Garner died in a chokehold, before he said "I can't breathe," when the police first stopped him he said, "Every time you see me, you want to mess with me. I'm tired of it."

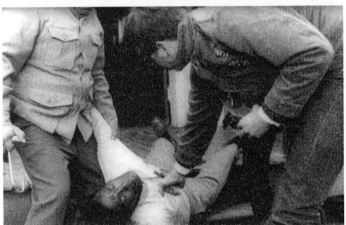

Night of the Living Dead, *dir. George A. Romero, 1968*

George A. Romero might have inducted the zombie into the annals of horror movie monsters forever, but in *Night of the Living Dead* (1968), what was far more unbelievable (and radical) is that the lead, the hero, the man in control of the situation, is Black. He spends the film telling white people what they should do, calming them down, he even slaps a hysterical white lady in the face. Trapped inside an isolated house in the country, the white folks are either catatonic, weak, or selfish. Ben (Duane Jones) is smart, decisive, and brave in his heroic efforts to save the lives of these strangers, but having survived a night of an invading horde of the walking dead, having protected a group of white men and women from being eaten alive, as he walks out of the house in the light of day, the police immediately shoot him, assuming he is a zombie.

The end is shot in a montage of still, black-and-white photos and resembles a documentary more than a horror film. They stab his body with a hook to more easily drag him to a pile to burn with the rest of the monsters. While the zombies may have been relentless in their pursuit of human flesh for food, they are innocent in their blind instinct. The police shoot first and don't bother asking questions later. Despite exhibiting none of the tell-tale signs of zombification — the slow gait, the moans, the dead eyes and decaying flesh — the police see a Black figure and automatically see danger. Before Jordan Peele won an Oscar for Best Original Screenplay, the Golden Globes, in a condescending tone-deaf act, nominated his film for Best Musical or Comedy. Peele's response: "*Get Out* is a documentary."

The conversion from personhood to commodity was just

the first step of the process of monsterization. What Frank B. Wilderson calls "social death," is a process of social zombification. The Black body (not Black person, but body) is susceptible to violence without reason, degradation without ramification, and available for exploitation. The monster is despised and feared by the very nature of its monstrosity. The monster is dangerous and threatening and therefore can be tortured, killed, or maimed with impunity. It may sound like I'm equating monstrousness with Blackness. I'm not. What I am saying is that the process of dehumanization is a process of monster-making. But monsters have power.

In Bill Gunn's 1973 film *Ganja & Hess*, we are introduced to anthropologist Dr Hess Green (also played by Duane Jones) in the backseat of a Rolls Royce, with his hand to his head as if he's ill. In a voiceover his chauffeur says, "He's an addict. He's not a criminal. He's a victim. He's addicted to blood." Dr Green had been stabbed by his assistant George Meda (Bill Gunn) with a dagger cursed by an ancient African tribe of blood drinkers, but don't call Hess a vampire; he's a man suffering from vampirism.

After transferring the curse to Dr Green, Meda commits suicide and his wife Ganja (Marlene Clark), is left widowed. Initially she's horrified when she discovers her dead husband in the freezer and after some deliberation tells Hess a painful story from her childhood. After an epic snowball fight with a group of kids, her mother accuses her of being a slut for running around with a boy. Despite her insistence that she had done nothing wrong, her mother refused to believe her. Ganja says:

It was though I was a disease. I came down with Ganja, you know. And I think that day I decided that I was a disease and I was going to give her a full case of it. That whatever it was I was, she was gonna have it. That day I decided that I would provide for Ganja, always, do whatever had to be done, take whatever steps had to be taken, but always take care of Ganja.

After Ganja discovers that Hess is addicted to human blood, he asks her, "The fact that you think I'm psychotic doesn't frighten you?" Ganja says with a smile and a shrug, "Aw man, *everybody* is *some* kind of freak." She decides to marry him, and his money, and agrees to become a vampire like him and live forever. Hess, riddled with guilt, kills himself, but Ganja lives on fully embracing her immortality, her freakiness, her monstrosity, and her power.

Being the monster allows for a unique ability to see in the dark. The other has the clarity and awareness that fear obscures. To be the thing that strikes fear in the hearts of men is to know more than they do, to know them more than they know themselves. It's dangerous, and to be sure, the villagers will always be at the ready with their torches, but the monster lives where you are afraid to go, it watches you while you sleep, hides in the shadows where you can't see, it poisons the master's tea when they're not looking. The monster knows what you did last summer. America has gotten away with murder for four hundred years, and it's been sleeping with one eye open ever since.

BLACK IS THE COLOR OF MY TRUE LOVE'S HAIR

There is no "very black." Only white people use this term. To blacks, "black" is black enough (and in most cases too black, since the majority of black people are not nearly so black as your black pocketbook). If a black person says, "John is very black," he is referring to John's politics, not his skin color.
— Fran Ross, *Oreo*

I didn't know him, but he looked like someone who might have gone to our church: a Black man in his sixties or seventies, someone I would instinctively call "Sir." He pointed at my t-shirt which read "Black Celebration 1986" in bold black, yellow, and red type. He nodded with an impressed smile, and I basked for a moment in the warm approval of my elders without knowing exactly why. He said, "Yes! We *should* celebrate." I nodded and smiled with a meek, "Yeah." "Is it a special event?" he asked. Confused, I answered, "I guess? I mean I've seen them before…" It was his turn to look confused and then it clicked. "Oh, it's a band." I turned around showing him the back with the Depeche Mode logo and the tour schedule. "Ahhh," he nodded then asked, "Are they Black?" I could anticipate the disappointment and when I quietly answered, "No." His face dropped a little and whatever Black-folk bond we shared at the moment dissolved as we realized we were not celebrating the same kind of Black. Suddenly the song felt offensive to me, yet another example of black as a metaphor for something awful, with its oxymoronic title: a toast to the end of "another black day," because a black day is never a good day. As someone who has always been attracted to the dark side, as a night person who thrives after midnight, as someone who prefers the shadows to the spotlight, the negativity of black has always been a positive and my Blackness didn't have anything to do with that.

Over the years my closet has become blacker and blacker, to the point where it's now something of a textured void: a row of black fabric of various shades, temperatures, weight, materials and textures. If I'm not wearing black then it is decidedly NOT black: white, because of its non-blackness, or chambray for its proletariat neutrality. There has to be a reason why I would not choose black, and that reason is rarely good enough. Grey is sometimes OK.

I may have a gothic heart, but I'm also a creative director in New York City and black has been established as symbolic of a kind of management of the arts — the human equivalent of the gallery's white box. The all black outfit has the quality of an authoritative uniform of consistency and simplicity. If I could get away with it, I'd wear a Jesuit cassock every day.

Fashion designer Yohji Yamamoto said, "Black is modest and arrogant at the same time," and it's a description that feels uncomfortably suited to me. I think it's impossible to wear all black all the time without a smidge of superiority. Black is staple of such authority it has become the standard by which all colors aspire to. The phrase "[something] is the new black" means to be the new classic, the new basic, the next necessary thing. The color black signals a kind of unaffected cool, a latent self-possession that is at once alluring and intimidating, something carefully considered and effortless at the same time. Blackness, for the same reasons, is codified as cool, signaling a hipness that since white people started going to jazz clubs in Harlem has been co-opted and commodified for non-Black consumption. Blackness on non-Black people signals a pretense of outsider rebellion and anti-establishment bravado.

Détroit is the New Black, founder Roslyn Karamoko, logo by Bellweather

Black contains multitudes... literally. As a pigment it is all colors all at once, but black is also the complete absence of all light. Black is nothingness, absence, a void, the abyss. It's everything and nothing at the same time. Black is the color of omission — the black outlines of redacted classified documents, the strategically placed black bars covering nipples, the lost time of the blacked-out drunk. Black covers up, hides and deletes. Black courts suspicion.

U.S. Department of Justice
~~Attorney Work Product // May Contain Material Protected Under Fed. R. Crim. P. 6(e)~~

Harm to Ongoing Matter

[redacted]

30

Redacted text from Report on the Investigation into Russian Interference in the 2016 Presidential Election, Volume I *by Special Counsel Robert S. Mueller, III, March 2019*

On the flip side, white is symbolic of a kind of moral purity and virgin innocence. If darkness is indicative of evil, light is its opposite — everyone knows that the White

Hats are the good guys and the Black Hats are the bad guys. To be en*light*ened is to have knowledge, awareness, and clarity. It has spiritual connotations of reaching a more evolved level of consciousness. Dark is the absorption of everything, weighted down by sin, melancholy, and secrecy. To be "in the dark" is to be in a state of unknowing and ignorance.

Most pertinent to the gothic, black is a signal of death (in the West at least. In most of Asia, white is the symbol of mourning). The color of the Grim Reaper's cloak, the great plague, and the color of the ravens and crows that come to pick bones dry. Black is the color of ninjas, cat burglars, and pirates. It is either a melancholic or maleficent chroma, or sometimes both simultaneously. Black is the color of mystery and shadows, and the children of the night only make music when the sun goes down.

The image of goth as a subculture is a palette of black clothes and white skin. Despite the brown and black influences that run through the cultural gothic spectrum (Mexican Día De Los Muertos, Afro-Caribbean hoodoo, and Ancient Egyptian symbols of the Dead), goth is perceived as Caucasian culturally and aesthetically. But I recall Egyptian ankhs and scarabs being just as popular an accessory as crucifixes and pentagrams. Goth borrows and samples from the ancient and the archaic regardless of religion, culture or ethnicity, but its reputation is that of a black on black wardrobe with a tubercular complexion.

The whiteness of goth is in its excess of paleness, the cool pallor of a life spent indoors or under overcast skies. The blinding vampiric white makes black so much blacker. It is a palette of extreme contrast with none of the meek dilution of pastels or the warm comfort of browns. The idea of white skin and whiteness is so meshed with the gothic that the translation from whiteness to Blackness is sometimes an awkward one.

Black goth blogger Dana Dillipede asked in a post, "Does pale foundation mean one is ashamed of their skin color?" The general response from readers was for the most part "you-do-you-isms," and much like the debates over natural versus straightened hair, in one corner some say it's nothing more than a style preference and aesthetic choice. In the other corner, relaxed hair, weaves, and foundation a shade lighter than it should be means succumbing to hegemonic standards of white beauty and is symptomatic of self-hatred mired in colorism.

One Halloween, I attended an office costume party as a "person in a black-and-white movie" à la *Pleasantville*. My clothes from head to toe were various shades of grey, as was my make-up (grey foundation, grey eye shadow, grey lipstick…). I wore a black skirt with a white shirt and grey cardigan with my chunky black glasses and a black bob wig that covered up my naturally brown ears. I looked awesome if I do say so myself. A white co-worker came up to me and whispered, "That's not very PC of you." I replied with a confused "huh?" and she said, "Dressing up as a white person for Halloween!" Several thoughts went through my mind: does this person think I'm either insane or stupid enough go to an office party in a "white person" costume? Since when is grey a normal human skin tone? What else was reading "white" to her? Was it the cardigan? I decided to compromise and told her I was a zombie librarian. In the case of goth, it's the intent that matters. Are you trying to look white or are you trying to look dead?

Punctuated Blackness, 2013, 8.5" x 14"
(archival inkjet reproduction of woodblock print)
All images courtesy of Kameelah Janan Rasheed

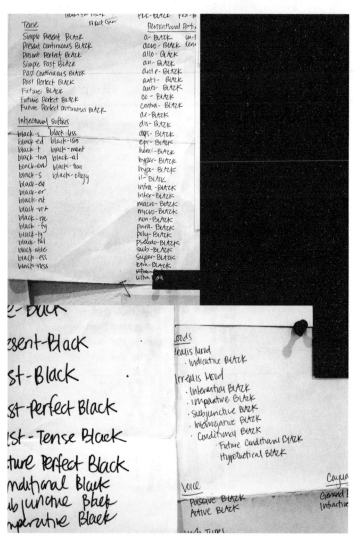

Installation Shot from No Instructions for Assembly, Activation VII, 2015

(photograph)

All images courtesy of Kameelah Janan Rasheed

The Invention of Blackness

The word "melancholy" comes from the Greek "melan" meaning "black" and "kholē" meaning "bile." It has its origins in the fifth-century Hippocratic theory of humorism, the belief that health could be dictated by a balance of humors flowing through the body: blood, yellow bile, black bile and phlegm. Black bile was considered the "melancholic" humor and was attributed to moroseness, fear, and prolonged sadness. But unlike blood or phlegm, black bile has no basis in anything biological. It's a substance of pure affect, not of mucus or plasma. Sadness created its own stuff. One particularly disgusting theory claimed black bile was the result of decomposing flesh released into the bloodstream resulting in a spectrum of ailments: headaches, vertigo, paralysis, epilepsy, diseases of the kidney and spleen. The "negative" emotions like introspection, sentimentality, excessive grief, loneliness, alienation, misanthropy, and cynicism were attributed to too much of the black stuff.[1]

Black is a color, a mood, and a state of being, and all of these attributes contribute to the construction of Black as a race. Black does not exist in nature, it had to be invented — black had to become Black (or negro or colored or darky or spade). Even the phrase "person of color" assumes an identity according to hue: something "not white."

The invention of Blackness was a crucial marketing tool of chattel slavery. To justify the buying and selling of human beings, the enslaved had to be diametrically oppositional to the slavers, all the way on the other side of their cultural chroma. If the only thing separating one human from another is the tone of their skin, that tone must carry an excessive level of contrived meaning. The Age of Enlightenment saw the birth of both the gothic genre and the classification of race and while one delighted in chaos, the other craved order. One embraced the dark and the other reviled it.

In 1767, Swedish naturalist Carl Linnaeus wrote *Systema Naturae*, in which he created a color-coded taxonomy of humanity. Each continent had a color and designated humor with conveniently specific attributes: Europeans were white, sanguine, and gentle; Native Americans were red, choleric, and obstinate; Asians were yellow, melancholy, and severe; Africans were black, phlegmatic, and negligent. In 1775, Johann Friedrich Blumenbach wrote *De generis humani varietate nativa* (*On the Natural Variety of Mankind*), which divided human beings into five races: Caucasian, Malaysian, Ethiopian, American, and Mongolian. He touted monogenism, the belief that all races came from a single origin (white), but that environment and poor diet would result in the degenerative darkening of the skin. Eighteenth-century surgeon Charles White thought that whites and Blacks were entirely different species. The assumption of whiteness as normalcy placed anything not white not only as inferior and unformed, but something all-together other, and America has never entirely debunked this fake science.

This "phantasmatics of colors," as Alain Badiou calls it, was legitimized by the pseudoscience of human biodiversity, which allowed the purveyors of the slave trade to treat Africans inhumanly because they were determined authoritatively to be not-quite-human. To sustain the cognitive dissonance required to buy and sell, and in the process, physically and psychology torture human begins, the nature of Blackness had to be genetically adapted for servitude. Blacks were believed to have a higher tolerance for pain (a myth that persists to this day), to need less sleep, and to lack the sentiment and ability to appreciate or create art. It was determined that Blacks felt less physically and emotionally, so one could beat them because they could take it, and work them from sunup to sundown because they didn't require rest. To top it off, Black people lacked the emotional sensitivity and complexity that would suggest an interior life and a soul. The Black body "would not be slowed down or deterred by such human qualities as memory, longing, despair, or fear."[2] Less than an animal, the Black body was a machine.

Through the publications of biologists, anthropologists and social scientists, black became Black: a temperament, a pathology, an economic indicator, a quantifiable attribute, and a definable thing whose characteristics could shift and morph as needed. Black people are simultaneously lazy yet built for labor, childlike and in need of guidance but also violent and aggressive. The men are well endowed and the women sexually promiscuous. We like watermelon and fried chicken. We can sing and dance and excel in sports (except for swimming and skiing), but we don't go camping. We go to church, but not psychotherapy. We like Tyler Perry movies and Moscato... The more specific the list of attributes, the more defined the characteristic, the lesser the humanity. The lesser the humanity, the easier it is to abuse, patrol, ignore, blame, exploit, or kill. But the identity that we call "Blackness" is ephemeral and subject to ever-shifting adjustments of performance. There is no One True Black, but the undefined are unpredictable and harder to control. The undefined are more frightening.

In the effort to define Blackness as a methodology of control, Blackness also had to become strange as a method for dehumanization. For imperialist Europe, the Dark Continent was about as strange as you could get. By the late 1800s, Victorian explorers and missionaries traveled to Africa with aims of Christian conversion and economic exploitation. The bright, white light of civilization would shine on these dark, heathen savages whether they liked it or not. This correlation between light and dark, day and night, civilization and savagery persisted.

The light-skinned house slave vs dark-skinned field slave hierarchy has never been fully expunged from our culture. Spike Lee's *School Daze* takes place at a HBCU and centers around the conflict between the light skinned "wannabe white" sorority girls versus the dark skinned "jigaboo" Black activists. Back in the day, affluent Black churches, fraternities, clubs and social organizations used the Paper Bag Test as a caste system, separating the light elite from the darky riff-raff. If your skin was darker than a brown paper bag you were turned away at the door. The Blue Vein Test was another: the skin on your wrist should be light enough to show a blue vein — a painfully obvious nod to Anglo-Saxon Blue Blood affluence. These stringent practices may have died out in the 1950s, but in 2016, when actor Jesse Williams gave an impassioned speech about racism at the BET (Black Entertainment

Television) Awards, people questioned his authority to speak on behalf of Black people because of his light skin and blue eyes. It was thought that his privilege as a biracial man afforded him the respect and attention a darker-skinned man would never have. And the truth of the matter is that it does.

Darky

One of the simplest and most effective ways to evoke dread is to be plunged into darkness. The monster in the void will always be more terrifying than the one we can see: the emptiness of the open door in the middle of the night, the edge of the woods where the trees melt into the dark, the walk down into the blackness at the bottom of the basement. Nothing good is ever at the bottom of the basement stairs. We don't know what lurks in the shadows, and that void of unknowing is an uncomfortable space to inhabit. We are temporarily at a disadvantage and vulnerable to the thing we can't see but that can see us.

In 1757, British philosopher Edmund Burke published *A Philosophical Enquiry into the Origin of Our Ideas of the Sublime and the Beautiful*, and in doing so laid out the blueprint for the gothic aesthetic. He defined, with extreme specificity, those qualities that evoke a "delightful horror, a sort of tranquility tinged with terror." Pointy things are scarier than smooth things, quick furtive eye movements are disturbing, long hallways of archways that seem to go on without end, vistas obscured by mist and fog, those things whose borders have no perceptible edge, whose scope we can't see, are most frightening:

> To make anything very terrible, obscurity seems in general to be necessary. When we know the full extent of any danger, when we can accustom our eyes to it, a great deal of the apprehension vanishes. [Night] adds to our dread.

Burke had quite a lot to say about darkness, which, he claims, is not the same as blackness. Darkness, he says, is uncertain, terrible, and gloomy. However, "blackness is but a partial darkness. Black bodies, reflecting none, or but a few rays, are but as so many vacant spaces dispersed among the objects we view." Blackness is a piece of darkness in the midst of light, an absence of color among colors. To illustrate his point, he recalls the following anecdote (emphasis mine):

> Mr. Cheselden has given us a very curious story of a boy, who had been born blind, and continued so until he was thirteen or fourteen years old; he was then couched for a cataract, by which operation he received his sight. Among many remarkable particulars that attended his first perceptions and judgments on visual objects, it gave him great uneasiness; and that sometime after, **upon accidentally seeing a negro woman, he was struck with great horror** at the sight. The horror, in this case, can scarcely be supposed to arise from any association. The boy appears by the account to have been particularly observing and sensible for

one of his age; and therefore, it is probable, if **the great uneasiness he felt at the first sight of black** had arisen from its connexion with any other disagreeable ideas, he would have observed and mentioned it.

For Burke, the blackness of the Negro woman means she is both seen and unseen, a physical void, a material shadow. The project of dehumanization positions Blacks as something other than human and outside social recognition. To the non-Black boy, the Black woman is perceived as absence, a negation. Living, breathing, speaking nothingness. Blackness was not merely monstrous, it was phantasmagoric.

I prefer "Black" to "African American." The later excludes others of the diaspora living in America and has connotations associated with the descendants of slaves brought here from Africa. Not all Black people were slaves and not all Black people in America came from Africa. There is also a formality to it that smacks of the classification efforts in the eighteenth century. While Black people have fought hard, and are still fighting, to be seen as American, the moniker rings false to me, like it's trying too hard. Since the scientists of white supremacy decided that we had to be something else, since they had to become white in opposition to whatever it is that we are, the term kept shifting from the ones we were given to the ones we take for ourselves: nigger vs negro, African vs Afro-American, colored vs people of color. The one that remains through all the socio-political movements is "Black," and it is the one I prefer most for all of the reasons why I love the color black. It's clean and direct; there is nothing indecisive about black. Black is. It's strong (like I hope to be) and a bit aloof (like I sometimes am). I prefer Black because black contains multitudes. Because it is everything and it is nothing.

WHEN DOVES CRY

You are standing on the site where enslaved people were warehoused.
— The Legacy Museum in Montgomery, Alabama

Like a lot of Black people, I tend to keloid. I was so excited to finally get my ears pierced when I was thirteen and so dismayed to see the bumps that grew in their stead. A keloid is an overzealous scar that grows beyond the initial cut. In the process of healing, the scar extends the boundaries of the original wound, leaving a larger, more prominent and permanent trace that's bigger than the original wound. The evidence of the injury becomes an object in and of itself — its own mark, with its own issues that never lets you forget. It just keeps healing and healing and healing...

I hate the word "heal." It's part of the language of memorials and mourning, but it's too nice and passive, suggesting a gentle and natural repair. The phrase "open wound" is often used to describe the unresolved damage left from chattel slavery, and it's one with gory undertones. Heal, wound — these are words of the body that imply a physical injury, sliced deep through to the epidermis and muscle and into the guts, the kind of visceral damage that festers if left open and raw. The healing process from the wounds of slavery is more of a keloid to me. The original cut might have healed over, but something bigger and more resilient took its place, something that, over time, mutated into its own creature.

If the formula for comedy is tragedy + time, the same can be said for the gothic. The romanticization of the past can only occur long after the damage — time enough for the effect of mourning to become an aestheticization of melancholy. In the eighteenth century, the wealthy decorated their land with fake remnants of medieval ruins, but the architectural folly is not so charming if the battering ram came crashing through your front door. The culture of death that inspired the goth(ic) aesthetic came out of the Middle Ages when the Black Death killed hundreds of millions of people across Europe and skulls and skeletons made their way into art and objects. The Hundred Years' War killed millions more. When death becomes so much a part of the fabric of regular life it finds its way into the culture.

Dead Black bodies have always been part of the American visual landscape, from the postcards of lynchings to grainy police dashcam footage. Claudia Rankine writes, "The unarmed, slain black bodies in public spaces turn grief into our everyday feeling that something is wrong everywhere and all the time, even if locally things appear normal." If Black lives in the twenty-first century have anything in common with Europeans of the 1400s, it is an intimate relationship with death.

Death holds an uncanny position of being simultaneously the most common and the most mysterious phenomena in the human experience. It is both repellant and enthralling, and the gothic is balanced on the sliver of space between the two. Death is the nexus from which the gothic and horror is formed: facing the dread and terror of dying, exploring the mystery of what comes after, the rituals performed in the aftermath and all of its accoutrement — what Carol Margaret Davison calls "necropoetics." The secularization and rationalization of the Enlightenment meant that the surety of an afterlife in heaven was no longer so cut-and-dry, and so anxieties arose about death. This kind of doubt yearns for clarity and structure, and the monumentality of death requires a practice one can perform — and so mourning became "a more fraught process that would lend itself to melancholic excess."

The key to humorism was balance. The "excess of introspection" and a "maudlin demeanor" could be spewed, excreted and drained from the body. But a little bit of introspection and sentimentality could do a body good. Ideally one would have just enough gloom goop or just enough sorrow in your spleen to write a poem or paint a foggy landscape. Too much and one could become pathologically stuck in misery without escape, metaphysically constipated. By the eighteenth century, however, humor theory was losing credibility, and melancholia (which would later become depression) was regarded more as an affectation affiliated with intelligence, sensitivity, and refinement. There was dignity in affecting a world-weary ennui, and a "necroculture" around death as formed among the Graveyard Poets and Gloomths with their persistent case of the morbs.[1]

The way mourning and melancholy looked was part of the gothic and the goth. An aesthetic was formed around the materiality and performance of mourning, and mournfulness took on the air of romanticism. There is a difference between the performative, theatricality of gothic melancholia and clinical depression. It is a Theda Bara pantomime of sadness and an exaggeration of emotion. It's melancholy as camp.

Contemporized widow's weeds, elegiac electronic music, skulls as accessories, and languishing over graves that have been chosen based on the design of the headstone and not the person underneath, are part and parcel of the goth aesthetic. But it's not any kind of mourning; it's an Anglo-Saxon kind of despair. It's not the wailing cry and beating of breasts, or a celebratory processional; it is a silent mourning, one of slow moving gestures, a languishing culture, the back of a hand gently pressed to the forehead in pre-swoon, the cough into a gleaming white handkerchief revealing a bright red spot. Goth(ic) is a necrotic romanticism. It brings the spectacle of dread that is mourning, out of the context of the church, or graveyard, or funeral parlor and into the light of day. In his memoir, *Bad Kid*, David Crabb described seeing a group of goth kids when he was fourteen in his suburban Texas town: "Well, I'll be," my father sighed. "They look like superheroes going to a funeral." As much as it is a fashion, a color, or a music genre, goth is a pose and a posture.

If you ever find yourself in Independence, Missouri, I recommend a stop at Leila's Hair Museum (the name is purely coincidental). Located behind a beauty school in a strip mall, is a collection of hundreds of pieces of Victorian hair art, elaborate wreaths of intricately arranged hair as memorials to loved ones, including ones made from the members of the League of Women Voters from 1865. There are brooches with the locks of former beloveds and little scenes painted with trimmings of the hair of children who passed away too soon. Death decorated the walls of parlors, was encased in lockets, and woven into black-rimmed mourning rings worn by widows and widowers alike.

My mother is Black but has fair skin and straight hair and if you just glanced at her quickly you *might* mistake her for white. According to the Natural Hair Chart, my hair is a thick, kinky 4A and my mother's is a thin, wavy 2C. One day when I was in high school, I received a package in the mail. There was either no return address or I didn't recognize it, I don't remember which. Inside the package was a plastic Ziplock bag with a long, thick, braid of dark brown hair inside. There was no note. I was convinced I had an enemy somewhere who was putting some kind of hex on me, but a few days later I got a letter in the mail from my grandmother saying that she was sending me a lock of my mother's hair that had been saved from when she was a little girl. I'm not sure why she didn't think to send the letter *with* the hair, but that's neither here nor there. I still have it, a plastic baggie of my mother's hair. I feel like I should do something with it, make a wreath of my own, while she's still here.

Goths borrow bits and pieces from the uniform of mourning, creating their own forms from their own time, but they owe a debt of gratitude to Queen Victoria. After the death of her husband Prince Albert, she remained in full mourning gear for three years and a stylized system for mourning became *de rigueur*. The social rules of fashion and etiquette were entwined with the rituals of bereavement. This included heavy, black dresses, with veils made of black crêpe, special black caps and bonnets, and jewelry made of jet. Mourning stationery and pages printed with a black border, allowed for correspondence that indicated death without the need to say it. Mourning was made formulaic, predictable, and consumable, and with the help of cholera and typhoid, everyone was doing it. Time frames were established depending on the closeness of the relation, "deep" or "full" mourning transitioned to "half" mourning, in which clothes could be switched from black to grey or purple. The width of the black border on one's correspondence narrowed the more time passed. We are accustomed to talking about mourning as a narrative, a linear process of denial, anger, bargaining, depression and finally acceptance, by which the acute pain fades into an endurable ache and the jet black eventually fades to grey.

If mourning is procedural, melancholy is persistent. In mourning, the lost object is replaced by a new something or someone and that sorrow morphs, diminishes in intensity as something else comes in to help patch the hole. Melancholy, on the other hand, is a permanent state of mourning. Here, there is no replacement, no fade to grey, the lost object is absorbed into the self and we become simultaneously the mourner and the thing being mourned. We are the void we are missing. There is no start, no process, and no end. Melancholy wakes up in the middle of the story and just stays there. Melancholia is a kind of stasis of mourning with no subject, a negative space with no matching positive shape. With no place to go, with nothing to do, melancholy just "is." The lost object doesn't have to be a person. It can be a lost home, a lost language, a lost religion, a lost history. When that missing person, place, or thing is so far removed from its original form, so fractured and disseminated, when its existence is denied altogether, that lost object remains unknown and unattended and absorbed into the self and into the culture.

After slavery was abolished in 1865, the agricultural south was left without the free labor it depended on and freed slaves were left with little options to support themselves. With sharecropping, free Black men and women worked the same fields they did as slaves, but now as "tenants," giving a percentage of their crop to the white owners who often took advantage with high interest rates or by cheating them out of their fair share of pay. White supremacy was sustained by Jim Crow laws and red-lining which segregated Blacks from whites and restricted access and mobility. Systemic surveillance and over-policing had, and still does, put a disproportionate number of Black people behind bars for minor or made-up offences, and today the for-profit prison industry provides free manufacturing labor — in other words, slavery. Despite emancipation, Reconstruction did little to rebuild what was razed. The social and psychic damage that was caused never stopped, and the trappings of the institution remained in the Black Codes of vagrancy laws and indentured servitude. Its form continues to shape-shift and its name changes to decep-tively legitimate concepts like, "states' rights" and "law and order," or bureaucratic legalese like "eminent domain" or "gerrymandering." The result is a persistent open wound from continued oppression, dehumanization, and an absence of the opportunity to heal.

How can you mourn the dead when the mechanics that made slavery possible are still churning? How do you get over the death of something that is still alive? What we thought was turning out to be a neat scar, healing nicely in the presidential election of 2008, grew into an uncontained, lumpy monster in 2016.

Giorgio Agamben suggests that melancholia "offers the paradox of an intention to mourn that precedes and anticipates the loss of the object [...] an anticipation of unfulfillment and damnation [...] the capacity to make an unattainable object appear as if lost." Slavery left behind a legion of losses both corporeal and intangible. There are those that died in the crossing, those who were killed in bondage, those worked to death or murdered outright, the families whose ties were split, and genealogies severed. There are countless bodies, but among the missing are lost identities, languages, histories, religions, names, traditions, connections, potentials, and futures. Those are things which can't simply be tossed overboard or buried in the ground — things that can't be reimbursed for or repaired. For the descendants of chattel slavery, there's no telling what was lost because there is no telling what could have been had. Black people arrived in this country already in a state of absence, already bereaved.

If mourning is predicated on the loss of *something*, melancholia is missing what you never had. So, if there is a persistent state of mourning lingering in the sub-

(and-not-so-sub-) consciousness of Black America, how is that melancholy made manifest? Joy DeGruy defines the effects of this loss as Post-Traumatic Slave Syndrome: the resulting trauma of multigenerational systemic oppression of the African diaspora, a persistent hum of fight-or-flight in the background, new violence inherited from old violence, old oppression evolving into new oppression, and the dead rising from the grave over and over.

Hidden Graves

"Want to know the difference between a casket and a coffin?" I plowed ahead without waiting for a yes or no. "A casket is rectangular like this one. A coffin has that old fashioned tapered shape. After the industrialization of the funeral industry the anthropomorphic shape of coffins were thought to be too creepy. It reminded people that there was a body in there." For someone who thinks and talks about death as much as I do, I am horribly awkward at funerals, and I took my brother's silence as a reminder that this may not have been the best small talk before our aunt's funeral. But I think about death and mourning all the time and it's hard not to want to talk about it while I'm in the middle of it. I once met a woman who was planning her own funeral on Pinterest, the online dream-board of lifestyle aspirations used by brides-to-be everywhere. She said, "I don't know if I'm ever going to get married. I *know* I'm going to die." Inspired, I began my own end-of-life planning, and I find it calming and clarifying: making up music playlists, noting flower preferences and choosing the type of burial (natural, no embalming, in a plain pine casket). What would I wear? What would I ask others to wear in honor of me? What will be the last gesture I make in the world, what is the last thing I will ever say or do?

Freshly dug graves have the best dirt for making mud pies. When I was a kindergartener, my little friends and I sat along the edge of a six-foot-deep rectangular hole, scooping up handfuls of rich black earth and molding and patting them into flat round discs with satisfaction. I might have felt a little bit of guilt, that perhaps what we were doing was sacrilegious or disrespectful, but that was part of the thrill, to co-opt this sacred space for our own use. When we were done with that we took turns "playing funeral," in which one of us would lie as still as we could, next to a gravestone, while the others wept and mourned our untimely passing. I have been playing in cemeteries for a long time.

Since the Graveyard Poets of the nineteenth century, the cemetery has been, more than any other setting, the locus of dark romanticism — a landscape designed specifically for the contemplation of death. The cemetery provides all the pleasure of a park but without the annoyance of people. With its acres of trees, rolling hills, lakes and elaborate mausoleums, Green-Wood Cemetery in Brooklyn is my Central Park. Walking through the great gothic arches into my necropolis, my pace slows and I stroll with my hands clasped behind my back, taking in the air for my weekend constitutional. Like museums or churches, the cemetery demands a certain decorum, a slower pace and a softer tone. There are no joggers huffing past me on the left or lycra-clad cyclists zooming past me on the right. Evan Michelson once said that cemeteries are "the only place I could be alone and surrounded by people at the same time." I quite like that perspective.

There are now a variety of interesting ways to memorialize the dead, much of which have to do with cremains: ashes sprinkled into vinyl albums, packed into pods to grow sapling trees, encased in fancy glass dildos, or pressed into diamonds. The death-positive movement re-introduced to modern culture the death doula — funerals at home in which family members wash and dress their loved ones the way they did in the old days, before interning them in environmentally friendly bamboo caskets wrapped in naturally decomposing death shrouds.

As an ecologically inclined person, my initial thoughts were that it would be irresponsible to take up space in a cemetery plot and that there was a kind of antiquated hubris about a coffin. I should want something more efficient, something more modern. But I do want a headstone. I want a hunk of granite with my name and the dates of my life span underneath. I want goth kids forty years from now to lounge over my grave holding roses for self-portraits. I'm less interested in my immediate family having a place to visit me, and more inclined to think of my spot for the ages. It's antithetical to everything I stand for, but goddamn it, I want a rock in the ground with my name on it.

Along the 5th Avenue side of Green-Wood Cemetery, far from the main gates, away from the stately Gilded Age mausoleums, is a placard near a large boulder visible through the chain-link fence. It reads:

> Legend has it that, near this spot during our Colonial period, an African American named Joost dueled the Devil in a fiddling contest. When Joost triumphed, the Devil, in defeat, stomped his foot on a rock, leaving an impression of a hoof print. This rock, recently dug out of Sunset Park's ground, reminds us of the folktale of the Devil's Footprint.

I came across this completely by accident having gotten off the bus a stop too soon. It's not the location that bothered me, or the fact that I've never heard the story before. It was the vagary of it all. It wasn't REALLY the rock, just one that looked like it. It wasn't the EXACT spot, just somewhere near there. It's almost apologetic in its timidity.

The legend goes that Joost (who may or may not have been a slave), was walking home from a wedding one night after one too many glasses of schnapps. He paused to rest on a rock and while admiring the starry sky he took out his fiddle and began to compose a tune. Engrossed in his playing, he failed to realize that the Devil had joined him, who then challenged Joost to a fiddle contest. Joost prevailed and the Devil stomped his foot in a temper tantrum and disappeared. The next morning, Joost found himself in a nearby field alone next to an empty bottle of schnapps. I wished there was a monument, something with some permanence, and a place worthy of a Black man with skills so good it pissed off Satan. There would be a fiddle etched into a grand marble obelisk above the words carved in Roman capitals:

JOOST
THE FIDDLER WHO SLAYED

But the dent in that boulder isn't really the Devil's footprint and the location is estimated:

IN THIS GENERAL AREA
(WE THINK)
A BLACK MAN FOUGHT THE DEVIL AND WON
SOMEWHERE AROUND HERE
(BUT NOT REALLY)

They say that death is the great equalizer, but some neighborhoods in Green-Wood are better than others. The Knickerbocker set of the Golden Age are buried here in monumental mausoleums along their own Park Avenues, with crypts the size of studio apartments. How you died was a reflection of how you lived, and as in life, the residences of the poor and disenfranchised are the first to be paved over in the name of development.

In August 2017 in Green-Wood, the graves of eighty-three African Americans dating back to 1858 were discovered in a sparsely populated area, close to the street and far away from the best neighborhoods.[2] If Boss Tweed and Louis Tiffany have their final residence in the Upper East Side of the cemetery, The Colored Lots, as they were known, were the slums. They were the cheapest lots, built with no foundations so that over time the headstones sank into the earth and disappeared. With no one visiting them and no one maintaining them, the names and birthdays and deaths were left to fall into oblivion.

Stories like this pop up now and then as the city tears down and builds itself up over and over again. A Black burial plot from the seventeenth century was found under the 126th Street Bus Depot in Harlem.[3] An incredibly well preserved Black woman in an iron coffin was discovered in Newtown, Queens.[4] The bones of slaves and servants are discovered, construction is halted, and the dead are recognized three hundred years too late.

Across the street from the Brooklyn Public Library's New Lots branch, is a charming, white clapboard Dutch Reformed church, with a sign on the front lawn reading, "All Are Welcome." The adjacent churchyard was neatly kept with crooked grey tombstones marked from the 1800s. Under the New Lots Avenue street sign was an additional sign reading: "African Burial Ground Square." I went across the street into the library to see if anyone there had any information about the graveyard and the librarian said, "Those were the officers and soldiers from the Revolutionary War. The slaves are under here." I instinctively looked down to the floor as if I would be able to see through the tiles, into the basement and through the concrete foundation to the bodies below. But there was nothing to see, just the speckled floor and the clarity that we're walking over the anonymous dead all the time.

The most prominent of these sites is the African Burial Ground, located at 290 Broadway in Manhattan, two blocks away from City Hall. The area is dense with office buildings, courthouses, banks, and shops, not too far from Wall Street and the site of the World Trade Center. It's on a nondescript side street that was intended to be the site of a new federal building and it's hard to determine who is infringing on whose territory. Such as it is with posthumous memorials, they have to share space with whatever is built on top of them.

Discovered in 1992, the remains of about four hundred and twenty Blacks (free and not free) were buried in what was, in the 1700s, known as the Negro Burial Ground. The entire burial site covers about seven acres, with an estimated fifteen to twenty thousand bodies, but the memorial itself only takes up about a third of a block. Soon after the remains were discovered, questions about how the site would be memorialized arose and an international call for entries went out for artists and designers to propose concepts. I don't remember much of the other entries but I do recall a lot of waterfalls. There was one proposal I really wish would have won. The artist (who I think was from Switzerland or the Netherlands) proposed that in every elevator, in every building on top of the entire seven acre site, well beyond the excavation, would be a plaque that read:

YOU ARE NOW SUSPENDED ABOVE THE AFRICAN
BURIAL GROUND.

That's it. A lovely little shove out of the historical amnesia that we experience every day, and a reminder as we float above Starbucks and the Stock Exchange, of the spectral undercurrent of Black and brown blood that built this country. It is not meant for quiet contemplation, it's not intended for those in mourning to pay respectful tribute. It's for the people who walk by the memorial every day without giving it a thought. It's uncomfortable and awkward. It's not a site for healing. It's a condemnation.

The project was ultimately awarded to Rodney Leon, a Black architect, and the design is pretty much what one would expect: uplifting quotes in script typeface carved into granite and African symbols etched into walls. It's OK. Like most public memorials, the emotional stakes are too high, for cool objectivity and consensus beats out creativity. The most powerful and interesting part of the grounds are the seven rounded rectangular mounds over the surface of the grass. The remains were sent to Howard University to be examined and then reinterred in seven coffins on the site. Perhaps it's because it is so simple in form, so clearly and obviously graves, that I prefer this to the curved polished wedge next to it. Buff away the etched maps of Africa and the symbols, and the form of the memorial could be for anyone or anything. Those seven mounds could only be one thing and there is nothing symbolic about it. They are exactly what they look like: graves disrupting the landscape of commerce and the law.

A resting place is a liminal space in between this world and the unknown, where peace and quiet are supposed to be guaranteed. It's not only where the physical remains are found — the person below becomes the owner of that place. In these new-found burial sites, the bodies there remain unnamed and grouped into a generic category: Africans, slaves, former slaves, free Black people... The grounds fall short of sanctified, as they are swallowed by the infrastructure of the city, as addendums to street signage or plaques on the side of a building. The "Square" in New Lots is invisible, undefined as a vague area to commemorate this particular collection of bones, but the people themselves remain anonymous. Relegated to the role of the "landmark," the empty space itself becomes the object to mourn, a numinous territory where the boundaries of history bleed into the everyday. These commemorative spaces are intended to be places that allow the opportunity to mourn a loss, but it is a loss that is generations removed from the mourner. Not a person, but one's "people," symbolic of millions of lost lives accumulating in a massive absence of the unknown and unknowable. There is no long list of names carved into the stone like the Vietnam Memorial or the World Trade Center memorial. Just the representational dead like the Tomb of the Unknown Soldier. But names matter. "Bodies matter. Personhood persists where it manifestly no longer resides; the dead, as represented by their bodies, are somewhere and are something." [5]

The new world was built up around and on top of the dead, and as a result these reminders become disruptions of normalcy — temporary blips of reckoning. But these are still sanctioned sites, gated areas, and designated places of mourning. In March 2019, the block between Gates Street and Fulton Avenue in the Clinton Hill neighborhood in Brooklyn, will be known as "Christopher Wallace Way." Christopher Wallace, also known as The Notorious B.I.G. or Biggie Smalls, was the legendary rapper who rose from the streets of Brooklyn to become one of the most significant artists in hip-hop history. Biggie was shot and killed in 1997 and the significance of his loss is made evident by the larger-than-life visages painted on walls of apartment buildings and bodegas all over New York. Clinton Hill and Bedford-Stuyvesant have become whiter and whiter as rents go higher and waves of newcomers gentrify formerly Black spaces, but the traces of the dead are still there on the walls. You might be able to buy bourbon-fig-vanilla beard oil and a Japanese-fusion taco, but the wall outside still has a portrait of a dead young Black man.

Comandante Biggie!, mural by Sean Meenan, Lee Quinones, and Cern One, Clinton Hill, Brooklyn, photo by L. Taylor

Unlike the deliberate visit to the cemetery, these tributes become part of the urban landscape and as result the traces of the dead become part of the historical texture of the neighborhood. Black neighborhoods from cities all over the country are painted with portraits of loved ones, as well as fallen heroes like Malcolm X and Tupac Shakur — *memento mori* in spray-paint and brick. Since its rise in the 1970s, graffiti has always been a form of remembrance, a permanent demarcation of presence and identity to say, "I was here." With its own culture, terminology, and aesthetics, tagging is a method of immortalization for the disenfranchised, the forgotten, and those most vulnerable to violence and death.[6]

Public practices of mourning usually occur in a few select places: funeral homes, places of worship, cemeteries, and private homes. Once the ceremonial "event" of the wake, the funeral, the burial or cremation is over, mourning reverts back to a personal, private experience. The memorial mural expands the mourning process beyond the personal and into the public for as long as the mural is preserved, remaining in the social consciousness for years and providing a public record of the critical events of a community's history.

These public memorials are practices in claiming visibility and a conspicuous expression of humanity for a marginalized population that has been dehumanized by historic, social, economic, political and cultural forces. The public mourning site is even more significant when the death is the result of violence, particularly when that violence is enacted upon young, Black men whose deaths are either sensationalized, stigmatized in the media, or reduced to statistics. The mural allows for a positive reflection of the deceased and control over how they are remembered in the community, transforming "personal grief into shared public sentiment by serving as a vehicle for community affiliation and potential empowerment."[7]

The need to name the dead, to put a body in the ground

marked with stone, is necessary for the continuation of memory, of presence, and of humanity. And the right to memorialization, to who goes in the ground, has long been determined by who owns that ground. When walking through a row of headstones, I am aware that the space in front of each marker is that particular person's place — the physical space of the body in the box taken up in this 3x8 foot rectangular area. But these public artworks mourn deaths that are not just personal loses, but are the result of systemic violence and social injustice, loses that effect whole communities.[8]

Black men are ten times more likely to be murdered than white men in America, and fourteen times more likely to die from guns.[9] The deaths of Black men are blazed upon social media with more and more frequency, creating a visual deluge of crime scenes, witness videos taken on cell phones, school photos, casual snapshots of victims, and television interviews of outraged neighbors, community leaders, and activists demanding justice for the victim, accountability for the guilty, and gun control legislation. The private individual loss has a second public-facing identity that becomes a political statement and a bereavement for the whole, not just the one.

Say Her Name

I remember watching *Roots* on a little black-and-white TV in our kitchen. The mini-series, based on Alex Haley's search for his lineage, told the epic story of an African American family, starting from West Africa in 1750 to post-Civil War Tennessee. I was five at the time and the only part I can remember is the scene in which the overseer commands another slave to whip a young LeVar Burton until he accepts his new name, the one given to him by his masters: Toby. It is a relentlessly violent scene, and the crowd of slaves watching flinch at every crack. Burton dangles limply with his hands tied above, sweating, naked from the waist up. His eyes are closed with exhaustion as he gasps in between lashes, "My name is Kunta. Kunta Kinte." When he can't take anymore and responds with "Toby," he is cut down. The Black faces in the crowd behind him bow their heads in disappointment, demoralized by the choice between the death of the body and the death of identity.

In the *Narrative of the Life of Frederick Douglass, an American Slave*, Douglass recalls seeing his Aunt Hester whipped and renders the scene in dramatic, gory detail:

> Her arms were stretched up at their full length, so that she stood upon the ends of her toes. He then said to her, "Now, you d——d b——h, I'll learn you how to disobey my orders!" and after rolling up his sleeves, he commenced to lay on the heavy cowskin, and soon the warm, red blood (amid heart-rending shrieks from her, and horrid oaths from him) came dripping to the floor. I was so terrified and horror-stricken at the sight, that I hid myself in a closet, and dared not venture out till long after the bloody transaction was over.

This offensive language is edited out (I'm assuming "damned bitch"), denying the master his power to name her, to brand her in this way. We are told her name is Aunt Hester, but he doesn't give Colonel Lloyd the satisfaction of repeating his insult, refusing to defame her further.

It's the most basic technique of humanization, but an effective one. The "X" of Malcolm X is not only a refusal of the master's lineage, but a kinship with the scores of lost souls whose names were never known. To take away the name is to revoke personhood. Frankenstein was the doctor, his monster is nameless.

In the protests and marches of the Black Lives Matter movement you'll hear the call-and-response cries — signs and hashtags to "say his name" and "say her name." The protest song, "Hell You Talmbout," by Janelle Monáe, is a running list of names of men and women killed by police brutality and state-sanctioned vigilantism:

Sandra Bland: say her name!
Sandra Bland: say her name!
Sandra Bland: say her name!
Sandra Bland: won't you say her name?
Say her name, say her name, say her name, won't you say her name?[10]

To be "woke" is to see through the veil, and the phrase has become part of the social justice lexicon. Social consciousness makes the hazy translucency of the past transparent and in focus. While being "awake" signifies an unveiled awareness, Sharpe observes that a "wake" is also a vigil held for the dead. "Living in the wake means living in and with terror[...] Black people become the carriers of terror." The privilege of non-Blackness is the ability to keep the curtain closed without ramification, to choose to see one point of view without the other. The normality of the spectacle of Black death makes it even easier to ignore as just part of our media landscape. I came into work one morning, a bit sad, angry, and shook up after watching Philando Castile die. The video, which went viral, shows a police officer shooting into a car and a split screen of a woman in the driver's seat capturing the incident on her phone. Castile is slumped over, moaning, with his hand on this side, and there is a massive bright blood stain on his white t-shirt. The caption on the screen translates his girlfriend's words: "Oh my god, please don't tell me he's dead." A co-worker asked me how I was and I said, "Not great." She asked why and I was a bit taken aback. It seemed obvious to me, it was everywhere, and of course I would be upset. Who wouldn't be? But she had no idea what I was referring to. That morning, I laid in bed, my thumb swiping down and down and down past the videos of dying black bodies and weeping mothers repeated again and again as they were shared over and over, past another #name in my Twitter feed, another Rest in Power and another name to add to the list of names to say. My non-Black friends and colleagues remained oblivious, cooing over kittens sitting on dogs while I just watched an innocent man get murdered on Facebook, again. While we were staring at the same screens and looking out of the same window, I felt as though the curtains were only drawn back on my side.

Artist Kehinde Wiley's painting, *The Virgin Martyr St. Cecilia*, is inspired by the 1599 sculpture of the same name by

Stefano Maderno: a likeness of the body of Cecilia found in her tomb incorrupt and in this same position. Wiley depicts a young Black man lying on the ground; his head is turned away from us and his arms are stretched out awkwardly underneath him. His hair is braided back in corn rows and he wears a bright orange hoodie, grey jeans and trainers. There is a pattern of pink flowers that surround him. Everything about the pose suggests a body that has fallen and never moved; it is a pose suggesting a sudden death, not a languorous repose. It is a pose that is seen more on the streets under flashing red-and-blue lights than in an artist's studio, and one expects to see a pool of red flow onto the white flower strewn cloth. It is a grand romantic image — a glorious depiction of an undignified death.

Affective Activism

It is amazing how something so brilliant can come out of such a mediocre building, but Paisley Park, the former recording studio and offices for Prince, in the suburbs of Minneapolis, Minnesota, resembles nothing but a generic corporate building. It's a sprawling complex of gleaming white geometry that seems designed to be purposefully innocuous. Once inside, we relinquished our cell phones and were led to the atrium to start the tour. Surrounding us was the balcony of the second floor, the ceiling painted in a Nineties *trompe l'oeil* of a blue sky with puffy clouds. On a small platform attached to the second-floor balcony was a scale model of the building which looked even more generic at that size. It seemed an odd place to put it —

something you'd usually find in a plexiglass box in the lobby. After a brief introduction to what we could expect on the tour, the guide then pointed up towards the scale model, revealing that it contained Prince's cremains. There was a resounding gasp, as none of us were prepared for that bit of information, and we bowed our heads in a moment of silence. Then I heard the burst of a gasp behind me and turned slightly to see a middle-aged Black man emit a loud guttural sob. He began openly weeping and one of the employees came over, put her arm around him and handed him a box of Kleenex. I glanced behind me, hoping to catch his eye, give him a solemn nod of solidarity and empathy, but he never saw me.

Crying is featured a lot in Jordan Peele's *Get Out*; in fact two of the most iconic scenes in the film are close-ups of Black faces struggling to fight back tears. Chris (Daniel Kaluuya) is visiting the family of his wealthy white girlfriend Rose (Allison Williams) at their large house in upstate New York. Feeling isolated and alone, he seeks connections with the few Black people he sees, such as the staff, but something's not quite right with them. The mutual nod of recognition you do when you see a Brother or a Sister isn't returned and they seem disturbingly content in their subservience. Someone keeps unplugging his cell phone and when he asks Georgina (Betty Gabriel), the housekeeper, about it, she brushes it off. Not wanting to get her in trouble with the boss, he says, "All I know is sometimes, if there's too many white folks, I get nervous, you know." Georgina's normally fixed grin falters slightly and she strains to keep the smile in place. She repeats "Oh, no. No-no-no-no-no-no," while a tear eases its way down her cheek, forcing its way through.

In the pivotal scene, Chris finds himself surreptitiously hypnotized by Rose's mother (Catherine Keener) under the guise of helping him to quit smoking. She hones in on his memory of his mother dying when he was a child and his inability to save her. His body is fixed to the chair, unable to move, and he strains to look away from her steady gaze as his tears are forced from him. In this psychic invasion, his personal anguish is turned against him. He shakes his head and as the tears run down his face his consciousness is repressed deep into a black void called, "the sunken place." With his mind, spirit, memory and identity (whatever you want to call it) buried deep, his body is free to be auctioned off to the highest bidder. Wealthy white people will use his Black body for its youth, virility, strength, and health. (Hence the particular affront to smoking. Some old, rich white man is going to be using him, so he better be in good condition.) We learn that Georgina, the Black maid, is really Rose's grandmother using the body of a younger Black woman as a vessel to keep on living, cooking, and taking care of her family — immortality through bodily possession. The Black body has value, the Black mind is disposable. As with Georgina, her tears are the last remaining bits of herself spilling out of the body as proof that she still exists.

Imagine, for a moment, that you've been kidnapped, that people who looked like you, who spoke your language, captured you and delivered you to people who did not look like you and did not speak your language. Maybe your wife or husband, your son or daughter, your best friend or your neighbor were captured too, but you end up in separate places. You are forced into the hull of a ship chained next to people, packed together. You don't know how long you'll be there, but eventually you get used to the stench of shit and piss and vomit in the sweltering heat. Despite all this, despite the hunger and the thirst, despite the diseases that spread from one to another, despite being kept chained next to the corpse of someone who succumbed, you don't throw yourself overboard in an attempt to kill yourself. After months, you finally land in a country you've never been to, are herded and examined like livestock, collared around the neck to a pole connected to six or so others like you, and made to march. Imagine you're nauseous or on your period or have a migraine. You're probably in shock. I hope you'd be in shock. The last thing you'd feel like doing is smiling and dancing, but when that journey brought them to the auction block, that is exactly what they were meant to do, to perform contentment in an act of salesmanship. I can imagine grins frozen in terrified rigor or repressed rage, eyes wet with tears or dulled from exhaustion. Black bodies are denied the humanity of emotivity. The cliché of the stoic Black man that never smiles, that suppresses laughter, is a conditioned response to centuries of cooning, buffoonery, and benevolent subservience.

In Kehinde Wiley's video piece *Smile*, there is a grid of young Black men shot from the neck up, in front of a white backdrop. Facing the camera, they are asked to smile and then to hold that smile for an hour. First, the smiles are relaxed and natural (neither the Angry Black Man nor the Uncle Tom). However, after a while, the forced smiling starts to take its toll. The muscle strain begins to show, the jaws become taught. The eyes betray the smile, and something closer to despair slips through.

It's easier to purchase a person if you're taught that they like being slaves, that they are relieved to have *finally* been captured and have the chance to live and die under someone else's control. Slaves were supposed to be happier when they were put to work — like a working dog, they're more content when they are doing what they were bred to do. It's a twisted marketing tool, selling the lie that the slave's spectrum of emotions is shorter and simpler than that of white people. Thomas Jefferson wrote: "Their griefs are transient. Those numberless afflictions, which render it doubtful whether heaven has given life to us in mercy or in wrath, are less felt, and sooner forgotten with them." In other words, Black people didn't feel sorrow, or if they did, it didn't last very long.

The key methodology of supremacy is establishing that Blacks don't *feel* the same way whites feel. The erasure of interiority and emotive policing reassured slave owners that what they were doing was not inhumane because Black people weren't quite human. They didn't have the same range of affect, therefore, empathy becomes irrelevant. Saidiya V. Hartman quotes a nineteenth-century witness to a coffle: "Given that the poor negro slave is naturally a cheerful laughing animal, and even when driven through the wilderness in chains, if he is well fed and kindly treated, is seldom melancholy."

The refusal to "step-lively" in the commodification of

emotions is an act of resistance, to be, as Eva Tettenborn puts it, Purposefully Melancholic. To be visibly in despair, to weep or wail, to let tears fall and mouths droop, to stare into the middle distance in still silence, subverts the perception of the nature of Blackness as being compliantly cheerful. In this way mourning becomes an affective activism.[11] There is a danger in the overexposure of the bereaved Black person — the repetition and frequency becoming numbing, and negating the purpose, which is to evoke empathy and humanity[12]— but if the image of the weeping Black mother is part of the visual language of Black protest, none have had the impact of Emmett Till's mother.

In 1955, fourteen-year-old Emmett Till, a Black boy from Chicago, was visiting his great-uncle Mose Wright in Money, Mississippi in the heart of Jim Crow country. Emmett was an extroverted kid from the city, so before he left his mother sat him down and told him how to behave in the south: "If you see a white woman coming down the street, you get off the sidewalk and drop your head, don't even look at her."

Despite his mother's warnings, after buying two cents' worth of candy at the grocery store, Emmett (allegedly) whistled at a white woman. Four days later, her husband and his half-brother broke into Emmett's great-uncle's home in the middle of the night, dragged him from his bed by gunpoint and took him away in their truck. They beat him beyond recognition, shot him and threw his body in the Tallahatchie River, where he was found three days later with a cotton-gin fan tied around his neck with barbed wire.

Beyond recognition is a nice way of putting it. It suggests that the person still looks like a person, just someone different. Emmett's face was decimated and the only things recognizably human were his nose and mouth, both of which did not seem to be in the right place. That image next to the photo of his huge brown eyes and chubby cheeks makes it seem unfathomable that any sane human being could do this to a child. But to his assailants Emmett was never a child.

Mamie Till's decision to show the mutilated body of her son, as it was left, without reconstruction, without makeup, was a political act of resistance. She insisted on an open casket funeral saying, "Let the people see what I have seen." A glass top was added, allowing Emmett to be seen while protecting the mourners from the odor of decay. News of the lynching spread, and fifty thousand people came to pay tribute. Tens of thousands more saw the photographs of Emmett's face in *Jet*, a popular magazine for and by Black people, and later that image would become a call to action for the Civil Rights Movement. Almost as significant as the photo of Emmett is the photograph of Mamie. She is leaning over the casket, eyes squeezed painfully closed, with her mouth in a tight grimace. Her right hand is lightly touching the casket, but her left is clenching her stomach. Everything about her posture suggests physical pain as if she's been kicked in the gut.

Emmett Till's casket is on display at the National Museum of African American History and Culture (NMAAHC) in Washington D.C. It is easily one of the most emotionally charged pieces in the museum's collection and the story of its acquisition takes a rather morbid path.

In 2005, the casket was exhumed as part of a renewed investigation into his death, and the body of Emmett Till was re-interred in a different casket. Then, in July 2009, the manager of Burr Oak Cemetery in Chicago was charged with digging up bodies, dumping them somewhere else, and then reselling the plots. Emmett's grave wasn't disturbed, but during the investigation his original glass-topped casket was found rotting in a dilapidated storage shed. The casket was donated to the Smithsonian Institution where it remained in storage and unseen until 24 September 2016, opening day of the NMAAHC, and since then thousands of people have lined up to pay their respects, again.

The elegiac weight of the object is evident in the design of the display. Some exhibits are tagged with a black sign and a red border reading, "Images outlined in red may not be suitable for younger or sensitive viewers." This museum of Black history is peppered with them, and there is one in front of the Emmett Till exhibit. It's a slow passage to the casket, giving you time to work your way up to it. Just before the room with the casket, is a display of the article in *Jet* magazine and the images and words of his mother in large script letters on the wall. You're led into an antechamber with a video of a documentary before you reach the final space containing the casket. The room is purposefully neutral with low lighting and subtle wood tones, designed with the "superstitious respect and veneration for the trace." [13] The casket is raised on two levels of platforms and visitors file past one by one, pausing for a moment before continuing on to the next exhibit or taking a seat in front of the display for a moment — a strange simulacrum of the funeral experience, a funeral for a phantom.

If houses have ghosts, if walls can absorb the echoes of human pain and anger, objects like Till's casket must be haunted: the white wood absorbing the rage and heartbreak, not only from the mother, but from the thousands of others who touched it that day, and the millions more that would see the photo. In houses, the original inhabitants of that space depart, leaving the next residents to deal with the phantom trauma. The casket without the corpse is fetishized, becoming the body, becoming the object of loss representative of the death of all, not just the one.

I have countless photos of headstones and tombs that I've taken at cemeteries everywhere. When I visit a new place, along with recommended restaurants, bars, and museums I usually check out the local cemetery. I recently realized that I have been to more parties in cemeteries than funerals. I once went to a fancy affair inside an exceptionally large mausoleum at Green-Wood, where people dressed in gowns and suits, drinking cocktails and dancing to a swinging Twenties jazz band, as couples kissed in the nooks of the crypts lit by candlelight. As I rubbed my fingers over the names on the wall, sipping champagne, I wondered if ghosts ever haunt their resting place, and if so, what would they think of all this? Would they be cool with it or just think it was strange? The dates below the names were mostly from the 1800s, which seemed safely long enough ago to not be disrespectful, and I wondered how much time would need to pass until strangers may confidently drape an arm over the curve of my headstone for a selfie and dance on my grave.

SCREAMING IT TO DEATH

Blues could not exist if the African captives had not become American captives.
— LeRoi Jones, *Blues People: Negro Music in White America*

Rhythm is both the song's manacle and its demonic charge. It is the original breath, it is the whisper of unremitting demand. "What do you still want from me?", says the singer. "What do you think you can still draw from my lips?"
— Grace Jones, "Jones to the Rhythm"

I grew up not too far from Hitsville USA, the little house that gave birth to The Supremes, Smokey Robinson, the Four Tops, Stevie Wonder, and Marvin Gaye, among others. The father of one of my classmates worked for Motown Records and she bragged about meeting Prince and The Revolution backstage at his concert. The first show I ever went to was the Jackson Five Reunion Tour, a group event organized by someone's parents. But the first concert I paid for with my own hard earned allowance was A-Ha, the tickets purchased at the corner store with a few packs of Now & Later candy. In those days, our parents would drop my friends and I off in Royal Oak to buy posters and pins at Noir Leather, where they sold band t-shirts in the front and sex toys in the back. We flipped through racks of albums at Sam's Jams negotiating who would own what to share with the other. Sarah got Bauhaus, but she made me a tape, filling up the first side with, "Bela Lugosi's Dead," on repeat over and over and over again. We would spend hours after school listening to records, dying our clothes black, cooing over vampires, and asking the Ouija board about our fate and the fate of boys we liked.

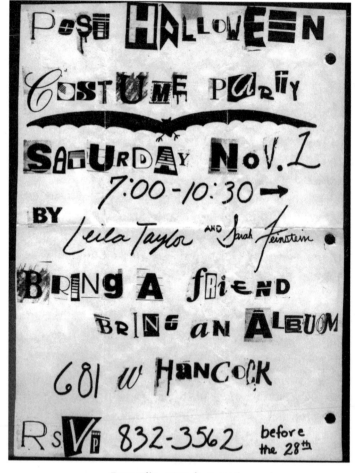

Party Flier, 1985, by L. Taylor

Our house on Boston Boulevard, was on the same street (albeit on the other side of the Lodge freeway) as Barry Gordy's, founder of Motown Records. I have a crystal clear memory of the dubious veracity of trick or treating at the Gordy mansion and getting a full-size Snickers candy bar, not the little fun-size. Legendary. When I aged out of trick or treating, in seventh grade, my best friend Sarah and I, co-hosted a Halloween party in the vacant half of her parents' two semi-detached houses on Hancock Street. Given full rein over an entire (nearly empty house), we draped the walls with black trash bags evoking giant bat wings and lit the living room by candle light (which in the hindsight seems incredibly irresponsible). We obtained, through great trials and tribulations involving a journey to a remote strip mall video store in the suburbs, a VHS tape of *The Hunger* which we played on repeat on a tiny television in one of the bedrooms, watching Peter Murphy back-lit with blue light behind chain-link fencing. The record player was set up below an antique candelabra and the next morning, to my dismay, I found my *Head on the Door* album by the Cure speckled with big solid white blobs. Heartbroken, I spent hours attempting to meticulously dig the wax out of the grooves with a sewing needle.

Growing up in Detroit gave me a musical advantage I didn't fully appreciate until I left Michigan, so I am one of the few people I know who can say they saw The Smiths live. It was my eighth grade science teacher, Mr Holstein, who introduced me to 102.7 WLBS Detroit's alternative radio station. They had a show that played new wave and post-punk music after midnight, well past my bedtime, and he taught me to set a tape recorder on my nightstand in front of the radio. I would be lulled to sleep by Tears for Fears and the faint mechanical hum of the tape recorder and in the morning, I would have a mix of Blondie, Talking Heads, Yaz, Soft Cell, Depeche Mode, Cocteau Twins, The Smiths, Siouxsie and the Banshees, and The Cure. To this day I consider "A Forest," to be something of a lullaby.

I used to feel that my inability to latch on to R&B, my dislike of saccharine love songs, my general indifference to hip-hop and rap, and my utter disdain of gospel music somehow made me less Black. I thought perhaps I was missing some genetic predisposition to melisma and that not liking "Black" music was somehow a sign of self-loathing and betrayal of my race, not yet knowing that the nucleus of all the music that I loved from those British bands, was located at the other end of my street where I once went trick-or-treating.

The Blues

I will be the first to admit, I don't know a lot about the Blues. It always seemed like music for white guys who wanted to seem cool, and as a youth I didn't know a single Black kid who listened to Blues albums recreationally. Jazz seemed cool and grown-up to me. The Blues just seemed sad. Ours was a Miles Davis / Barbra Streisand household with some Donna Summer and Stevie Wonder thrown in when my older sister was home. I had a jazz dad and a mom who loved opera and Willie Nelson. I also remember the soundtrack to *Victory at Sea* on heavy rotation and if I hear "Song of the High Seas," I get a pang of nostalgia.

One thing that was notably absent was gospel music. I was raised in the United Church of Christ, I was even in the church choir for a bit, but God wasn't around much in my house and going to church was more of a social obligation than a spiritual calling. On my confirmation day, I stood in front of the congregation in my new white dress with all the other thirteen-year-old girls in white dresses and gave my speech on what the church meant to me. Even then I knew I was feeding them bullshit, just saying what I was expected to say. When they handed me my own personalized Bible, my name was spelled wrong. I never believed in a supreme being or the resurrection, and it doesn't bother me in the slightest if we humans have no greater purpose. But I do believe that there is infinitely more out there than we know and will ever know, and I'm comforted by unknowing, I believe in doubt more than certainty. The UCC is a mild form of Protestantism with social justice as a main tenant, so there was never much need to rebel against it. The services are short and the sermons mostly amount to, don't be a jerk and if you can help someone whose less fortunate you should. We sing a few songs, buy a cupcake at the bake sale and then have brunch at the International House of Pancakes. There was no fire and brimstone so I never feared damnation, but I imagined if Hell did exist I'd rather go there since that's where all the fun people were.

Gospel music still doesn't stir me, but I have grown to appreciate spirituals, less for their "spiritualness" and more for the voices — the sounds of the past reaching out from the cotton fields and wooden porches. Spirituals always feel as though someone is trying to talk to me, to get a message through, saying "Don't forget me." Isabella Van Elferen describes sonic gothic-ness as 'the sounds of the uncanny,' a kind of aural haunting evoking a return of the repressed. I think of spirituals less as songs and more like ghostly communiqués.[1] The thinness of the voice, the degeneration and audio decay and these tinny, ghostly Black voices travel through time, whispering right into my ear through my headphones. I can see why Walter Benjamin uses the word "apparition" to describe this kind of temporal technological rift. An apparition is a ghostly vision, a phantasm, a disembodied spirit made present. Sound is a kind of touch and there is something a bit poltergeist-y about these warbling Southern voices creeping out of my speakers.

Spirituals and the Blues represent opposite ends of the Black experience: the spectral and the physical, the far away and the here and now. It makes sense that American music was born from these two sides of the veil, the pre-freedom longing for escape and the post-freedom realities of day-to-day life. The spiritual was an infusion of Christian music with African elements, music that was, as W.E.B Du Bois says, "adapted, changed, and intensified by the tragic soul-life of the slave, until, under the stress of law and whip, it became the one true expression of a people's sorrow, despair, and hope." Lyrics were both codes for emancipation in the real world and relief in the next. Spirituals were not entirely secular nor completely spiritual but both simultaneously. Eyes were lifted both toward Heaven and to Ohio, both on the River Jordan and the Underground Railroad. Living in bodies that did not belong to them, slave songs focused on the spirit, but once free, Black songs became very much about the body and the myriad of pleasures and problems that come with having one.[2]

At the end of the nineteenth century, Black gospel music was secularized into the Blues with themes of wandering women and cheating men, of being broke and broken down. The Blues luxuriates in feeling and the unabashed ability to *emote*. The misery and the sexuality of the Blues represents an affective freedom denied in slavery and dismissed in freedom. If a Black woman's heart can be broken, it means she had a heart to begin with and one can't help but luxuriate in the ability to wallow. The Blues was an expression of humanity and subjectivity and its performance was an act of sedition.

Strange Fruit

In the 1995 horror anthology *Tales from the Hood* directed by Rusty Cundieff, Martin Moorehouse (Tom Wright), a prominent Black activist is beaten to unconsciousness by police, and after realizing the trouble they'll get for brutalizing such a prominent and powerful person in the Black community, they kill him by injecting him with heroin to feign a drug overdose. Moorehouse rises from the dead to avenge his death by decapitating one and impaling the other with hypodermic needles. The soundtrack to the violence and revenge is Billie Holiday's "Strange Fruit."

I couldn't tell you how old I was when I first heard "Strange Fruit," but I must have been pretty little because I assumed it was a song about actual fruit and I thought Billie Holiday's voice was weird. She sang in a way that sounded too complicated or grown-up for me, like an R-rated movie whose references I didn't get and whose complexities were too mature for me to understand. She sounded like something was wrong with her. Of course, there was a lot that was wrong: she was an eleven-year-old girl abandoned by her mother, running errands in a whore house and pimped out by the age of fourteen. She grew up to die of alcohol and heroin abuse a decade before the Civil Rights movement. But in between those bookends she grew into an American icon without compare, giving the world some of the best music ever known.

I probably had a vague notion of who she was. I knew that she was important in some way for some reason that had to do with "my culture," but she was a fuzzy historical fact, a black and white photo of a smooth face with painted eyebrows. She was someone I should know, like Stokely Carmichael or Shirley Chisholm, but until I got a bit older she remained a frozen face on an album cover tucked away on my parent's shelf. I had a pretty advanced musical palette for a kid and I listened to and could appreciate music made before my time. I was able to form a narrative, however childish, around the artists that made the music and what it might have meant to them, if not to me. With Janis Joplin I could visualize a harsh and hardened life materialized from that gravelly Southern voice or the East Village artist's life from Nico's dreamy, drowsy German drawl. I couldn't see what created

Billie's voice. I couldn't locate the source of a sound that seemed so unfathomable. It was probably years before I heard it again. It took a second pass to get the metaphor and more time still before I would feel it, and see behind my eyes the grainy photos of ragged and bloody Black bodies suspended above a smiling white crowd. It was a while before the lyrics became material for me, the words so thick you could smell them. I also couldn't tell you the first time I saw an image of a lynching. It seems one of those things that I was just born knowing — something I've never *not* seen.

Abel Meeropol was a Jewish poet and card-carrying communist who wrote "Bitter Fruit" under the anglicized pseudonym Lewis Allen, after seeing a photograph of the lynching of J. Thomas Shipp and Abraham S. Smith. In the photo, taken on 7 August 1930 in Marion, Indiana, two Black bodies in ragged clothes hang from a tree above a crowd of white men, women, and children. Some are grinning directly into the camera, some are looking up at the hanging corpses and some aren't paying attention at all, as if the scene wasn't anything particularly interesting. Shipp and Smith were charged with the murder of Claude Deeter and rape of his girlfriend Mary Ball. The two were dragged from the courthouse by an angry mob, maimed, mutilated and hung in front of a crowd of five thousand people who came to watch the spectacle. By this time lynchings were decreasing in this county. Perhaps people thought of this as one last hurrah, a throwback to the old days.

From 1877 to 1950, about four thousand (that we know of) Black men, women, and children were lynched in the

United States. In a kind of mob vigilantism, Black people were abducted and murdered for trivial infractions or false accusations. It became a macabre form of entertainment, the kind that humanity has seen before, but can't seem to grow out of: the fascination with the destruction of the human body and the point in which a person stops being a person.

Photographer Lawrence Beitler sold thousands of copies of the photo in the following days. The lynching souvenir is a particularly disturbing artifact of an already disturbing practice. Like postcards of the Grand Canyon or snow globes of the Empire State Building, the photos prove that someone had been there. But what do you do with a photo of two dead men hanging from a tree? Are there thousands of scrapbooks in attics all over Indiana with that photo glued to the page? Did people put it on their ice box door with a magnet? Pieces of clothing and bits of rope were taken as keepsakes (no fingers, toes, or genitals were taken this time, but they often were.) I wonder about the granddaughter or great grandnephew decades later, home for Thanksgiving, finding an old stained bit of rope in the curio cabinet in between the Hummel figurines. Or maybe, like a novelty foam Statue of Liberty crown, it lasted a few days and was tossed in the trash after the thrill was gone. I can't decide which is worse.

In 1939, Meeropol put "Bitter Fruit" to music and Billie Holiday debuted *Strange Fruit* at the Café Society nightclub in New York City. As the city's only truly integrated club, it was an enclave for political radicals and progressive thinkers, but even in that environment, Holiday was hesitant to sing it, afraid that she'd never work again, or worse.

The story goes that when she finished singing, the crowd was dead silent, until one person began hesitant clapping. In my head, I see the classic slow clap... clap... clap as a single brave person rises slowly to their feet in ovation, then a few more join in and then more and the applause grow and grow... The song would become her signature and her performances were legendary. She always closed her set with "Strange Fruit," it was the last song of the night. Waiters, cashiers, and busboys all stopped service, and the room would be completely dark except for a spotlight on Holiday's face. At the Birdland nightclub in New York City, the maître d' confiscated all cigarettes before she started singing so there wouldn't be any extra light. When she was finished, the spotlight went out, she walked off the stage, and never went back to take a bow. Barney Josephson, the founder of Café Society said, "People had to remember *Strange Fruit*, get their insides burned with it." [3]

The effect of the song was devastating. Most of the audience at The Cafe Society never would have seen a lynching in person, but the Black folks in the audience were subject to all sorts of injustices, humiliations, and violence on a regular basis, and recognized the line between the rope hanging from the tree and the Whites Only sign on the door. They may have never seen it for themselves, but their parents might have. Their grandparents probably did. The white folks in the audience were never in one of those mobs, but their parents might have been, and their grandparents. People cried, then people got angry because Billie Holiday made them cry. It made people uncomfortable and the audience was made to sit and wallow in that discomfort. For the unaware it was a shocking awakening. For others it reopened old wounds. In later performances, it became customary to not applaud, denying that burst of relief signaling The End. It would have been disrespectful, like clapping at the end of a eulogy. The dramatic set up of the performance surely functioned as a kind of nascent trigger-warning, but I don't think anyone could be prepared. Listening to it now, in my home, with my headphones still makes me shiver. I can't imagine being at a table in one of the few nightclubs where I would have been allowed to sit at that table, a few feet away from Lady Day, witness to this euphonic indictment. In 2011, *Time* magazine named it the "song of the century."

But aside from the darkness of the theme and the gruesome lyrics, what makes "Strange Fruit" a gothic song? It's the contrast between the beautiful and the terrible (and I mean terrible in the classic sense to evoke terror), the scent of magnolias clashing with the stench of burnt bodies. The lyrics are both bucolic and grotesque, melancholic and horrific, enticing and repulsive, pastoral and visceral. And then there's the unique vocality of Holiday's voice. She sings from her head, it's shallow and seems a bit creaky, with unusual fluctuations of pitch and with sharp pronunciation of key words. The song is in B-flat minor, a gloomy key and ends on an unresolved F with a wavering, creaking, elongation of the word "crop." David Margolick, author of *Strange Fruit: Biography of a Song*, compares it to the dangling "dead man on the branch." Then, of course, there is the performance which is delivered with a ritualized drama and received with an almost religious reverence.

Claudia Rankine says, "Historically, there is no quotidian without the enslaved, chained or dead black body to gaze upon or to hear about or to position a self against." "Strange Fruit," no matter how many times it is sung, no matter who performs it, will always be positioned against the context in which it was written. Critics of "Strange Fruit" covers, often talk about the "displacement" of the song as an erasure of the political, sociological condition that created it, making it symbolic and transient. The cover song is always situated in comparison to a canonical version, the One True recording, and that version is always situated historically, leaving the cover vulnerable to temporal drift, re-contextualization and subject to new meanings and associations.

So, what happens when the song is shifted (spatially, temporally, culturally) from its original context: a Black woman singing in a jazz club in 1939 and relocated to an album by British post-punk band Siouxsie and the Banshees? What happens when Benjamin's "historical testimony," is deleted from the narrative? Positioned against other cover songs on *Through the Looking Glass*, it is reduced from a polemical indictment to a stylistic influence and an aesthetic atmosphere. It's normalized. As much as I love Siouxsie Sioux, in her hands, "Strange Fruit" is just not that strange.

Through the Looking Glass, is a collection of cover songs with artists like Roxy Music, Kraftwerk, and Bob Dylan. It also includes a sultry version of "Trust in Me" from the Disney film *The Jungle Book* (which has its own problematic colonial issues). I get why she covered "Strange Fruit",

I can understand how the song and the story behind it would be evocative and have meaning for Siouxsie Sioux, how Billie Holiday may have influenced her (she influenced a lot of people) and lyrically how it fits within the Banshees' wheelhouse. "The bulging eyes and the twisted mouth" sits comfortably next to Budgie's "pop eyed, horns, bushy tailed, long teeth and claws" of "Rawhead and Bloodybones".

Holiday's rendition is relatively minimalist in comparison. There's a long intro with a trumpet solo and then accompanied by the piano. The Banshees' version begins with the soft sound of whistling wind then dramatic violins interject in a classic horror movie soundtrack. A slow New Orleans jazz dirge is inserted in the middle with a little soulful "woo-woo," a little "performed anachronism" of Blackness to pad it with some authenticity. Just when you think it can't get any cornier, it ends with the sound of a distant bell toll. Siouxsie Sioux's rendition is actually more reminiscent of the idyllic antebellum South that the song denounces. It's closer to *Porgy and Bess* than "Cities in Dust." When she sings "Black bodies swinging in the southern breeze," I cringe, a bit embarrassed for her. These theatrical additives end up diluting, not enhancing the message. For an audience that may have never heard the original or recognize the metaphor, the song becomes just another example of spooky glamour in the Siouxsie and the Banshees repertoire.

I'm not suggesting that Siouxsie's version is less "authentic" than the Holiday version, but I am saying that it's a different song. The problem with remakes and covers of "Strange Fruit," is that it comes jam packed with a whole lot of meaning already and anything that complicates it further is doomed to fuck it up. "Strange Fruit" has been covered many, many times over the years by many different people, but there has always been some debate over who is "allowed" to sing it. Nina Simone's version was recorded in the Sixties during the height of the civil rights movement, which feels absolutely right. In 2015, Jill Scott sang it at a benefit concert called *Shining a Light: A Concert for Progress on Race in America*, so that makes sense. And even more recently, British singer Rebecca Ferguson publicly declined an invitation from President Donald Trump to sing at his inauguration, saying that she would perform only if she could sing "Strange Fruit."

For the record, I don't think it is inherently "wrong" for non-Black people to sing "Strange Fruit." I don't think it's wrong for Taylor Swift to do a country-western version of Earth, Wind and Fire's "September." I don't believe only Black Americans are allowed to sing "Strange Fruit." But recognizing the recontextualization that takes place with a cover, means recognizing that moving cultural artifacts from one time and place to another, risks erasing the artist and the story it was intending to honor.

Even though Siouxsie denounces the label goth, they are known as a quintessential goth band, and anything associated with that band is going to have a goth filter put over it. People buying the album are buying a Siouxsie and the Banshees album and unless the listener proactively searches out the original and its origin, the story of J. Thomas Shipp and Abraham S. Smith and the thousands of other victims, goes unknown, and the original tribute, honoring those swinging black bodies risks being lost.

There is a long history of Black music being remade by white musicians to make the songs and the artists who sung them more palatable to a white consumer audience, but "Strange Fruit" was never meant to be palatable... for anyone... Black or white.

Annie Lennox covered "Strange Fruit" on her album *Nostalgia* in 2014, which include such classics from the Black music catalog as "God Bless the Child," and "Summertime." I would like to ask her who exactly is nostalgic and for what? In an interview with the Black talk show host Tavis Smiley, Lennox said of her cover of "Strange Fruit," "[violence as a theme] is expressed in all kinds of different ways, whether it be racism, domestic violence, warfare, or terrorism, or simply one person attacking another person. This is something that we as human beings have to deal with."[4]

Annie Lennox never had to "deal" with lynching which she doesn't mention once in this interview. Insisting on a universality of "Strange Fruit" threatens Black erasure, taking Black Lives Matter and making it "All Lives Matter." It takes away the horror, the haunt, the discomfort that Billie Holiday and Cafe Society worked so hard to maintain. It takes away its bite and just makes it pretty. Van Elferen says, "The Gothic ostentatiously pushes the uncanny into its audience's face, demanding that they confront their own specters," which is exactly what "Strange Fruit" intended, and succeeded in doing. Taking away the Blackness of the song takes away its gothic-ness.

I resist the notion of thinking about "Strange Fruit" just as an old-standard from The Great American Songbook. It's not de-lovely or too damn hot and unfortunately remains too damn relevant. In November of 2018, shortly after the Midterm elections in the US, Republican Senator Cindy Hyde-Smith of Mississippi praised and thanked her friend and supporter, Colin Hutchinson, to a group of reporters and said, "I would fight a circle saw for him. If he invited me to a public hanging, I would be on the front row," evoking laughter from the crowd. Out of all of the states post-Civil War, Mississippi had the highest number of lynchings. 581 Black people were hung in public from 1882-1968.[5]

"The Passenger" is probably my favorite cover on *Through the Looking Glass* and like "Strange Fruit," I knew this version before Iggy Pop's original. It's an easy song to like; the lyrics are dreamy and hopeful with a danceable beat and sing-along la, la, las. But Siouxsie singing Iggy Pop is a lateral move. "The Passenger" doesn't have the weight of representation behind it and requires no authoritative voice to carry the heavy load of history behind it. "The Passenger" doesn't represent a people the way "Strange Fruit" does and it has the luxury of just existing on its own — light enough for anyone to pick up. Singing "Strange Fruit" requires the burden of speaking for legions.

The history of rock music is a history of theft, of white singers profiting from Black voices, stealing styles, picking up Blackness when it's popular and putting it down when it's not. In a way, the lyrics of "The Passenger" are representational of the privilege of their whiteness, and the need to claim everything:

And everything was made for you and me
All of it was made for you and me

'Cause it just belongs to you and me
So let's take a ride and see what's mine

I'm almost ashamed of my childish critique of Holiday, but I was a kid; I didn't know any better. I really hate to admit that I probably heard the Siouxsie and the Banshees version of "Strange Fruit" before Billie Holiday's, which is even more embarrassing since I was fifteen at the time and really should have known better. But I think it's because I skipped right over it most of the time. It was never one of my favorite tracks. The cultural erasure of the song muted it for me, made it something unrecognizable as something that was from my own story.

Now when I listen to Billie Holiday I know exactly where that voice comes from and it's not strange or wrong at all. It's exactly right and it seems preposterous to me that there could have been a time when I thought she was talking about rotten peaches. Now when I hear her voice and listen to those lyrics I don't see a "strange and bitter crop," I see Eric Garner face down on a sidewalk in Staten Island surrounded by white men in uniforms.

I Put a Spell on You

I went to New Orleans for Halloween and as my friends and I strolled along the parade on Frenchmen Street admiring the costumes, I saw a white man in blackface, dressed as some kind of "African Savage" with a leopard skin loincloth, a giant afro with a bone sticking through it, a spear in one hand and a red Solo cup in the other.

We were there for Anne Rice's Vampire Ball and despite spending most of our night in campy queer glamour, despite being in the protective comfort of my multicultural cohort of Yankee liberals, a wave of anxiety washed over for me as I remembered that I was in "The South." This is also why I have a complicated relationship with Screamin' Jay Hawkins.

Jalacy Hawkins, the godfather of shock rock and the forebear to Alice Cooper, Marilyn Manson, and Rob Zombie, wrote "I Put a Spell on You" in 1956 and claims that he was so drunk at the time he doesn't remember recording it. He intended for it to be a serious ballad, he was trained in opera and wanted to be a traditional blues singer, but what came out were the screams of wild man that didn't match the face of a suave crooner, and Screamin' Jay was born. When he recorded it the second time around he said, "I found out I could do more destroying a song and screaming it to death."[6] In his television debut performance on the *Merv Griffin Show* in 1966, Griffin introduced the audience to "one of the wildest singing gimmicks I've ever heard." Griffin said, "He may not scare you, but when he's performing you won't be going to the refrigerator." I'm not sure if that means the audience would be too enwrapped in the performance to take a snack break or if his performance would make them sick to their stomachs, but it's telling that he prefaces the act with the assurance that he *won't* scare them, that despite what they may come to expect, those in the studio audience were perfectly safe.

On the stage floor a skeletal, severed hand creeps its way through the curtains. Then the pompadoured Hawkins appears jumping over it, a cape flowing behind him shaking a tambourine in one hand and a staff with a skull with a cigarette out of its mouth impaled at the end. He punctuates the blast of the horn section with wild kicks and shaking legs, with a warbling "ooga-booga" chant like a schlocky B-horror movie version of a voodoo witch doctor. He looks around at the audience, wide eyed and confused as if he's not sure why they are there. There's nervous laughter from the audience as he hops bow-legged across the stage. He grunts, barks, howls, grumbles, and screams, the ramblings of a man possessed in some mysterious ritual from the darkest depths of Africa.

But there's this one moment where he appears to be on the verge of laughter himself, barely holding it in. It's a rock & roll cakewalk, making fun of white people's fears, giving them exactly what they thought Black people really were: savage, unintelligible, overly sexual, and scary. When he's done he gives a dignified bow and gracefully exits the stage reminding us that it was all an act. He was urged on by DJ Alan Freed, who convinced Hawkins to double down on the spooky imagery by rising from a coffin. He resisted at first saying, "No black dude gets in a coffin alive — they don't expect to get out!"[7]

The NAACP hated him. In the Talented Tenth rules of respectability, there is little space for the camp, the low, the ridiculous. Screamin' Jay Hawkins did not "uplift." Nina Simone uplifts. Her version of "I Put a Spell on You" from 1967 lifted it out of its vaudevillian gutter and into the sophisticated jazz club where Hawkins always intended it to be. It's a strange backwards evolution to take something originally performed as a novelty and treating it with gravitas; the words of a woman trying to reclaim the man who's been treating her wrong. It makes sense coming from Nina. It's played as a metaphor — what we want the song to be and what we expect a song to be. Her version is slow, raw, and sexy but without the speaking in tongues. It's the classy version.

Like Merv said, it's unlikely that anyone in the audience was afraid of Hawkins conjuring a spirit, or hexing them through the gamma rays and into their living rooms. It's more likely that they were afraid of being found out, of being exposed as people who deep down still believed that Black people went to witch doctors and shrunk the heads of their enemies. It's a fear of discomfort, like the audience at the Cafe Society, they were just there to have a good time, they weren't there to be schooled. Hawkins took full advantage of that discomfort by charging promoters an extra $5,000 to pop out of the coffin.

Screamin' Jay Hawkins was brilliant, and goth owes him a debt of gratitude, but I still get squeamish watching his performance. Was he a groundbreaking Black performer struggling to make it in a business owned by white people, fighting to keep his image under his own control, or would he forever just be a novelty act with his most famous song legitimized by other artists who played it straight (including Annie Lennox)? He resented being pigeon-holed saying, "Why can't people take me as a regular singer without making a bogeyman out of me?"[8] The performance, the visual presentation, the power of drama surpassed the song, assigning an identity for the artist that he couldn't shake. He screamed and so he became Screamin.'

I saw Bauhaus play at Coachella in 2005. Peter Murphy, still rail thin and vampiric pale, his spikey mop of black hair was now white as he sang, "Bela Lugosi's Dead," suspended upside down like a bat. It was fantastic and just the right amount of theatrics. Bauhaus became the goth archetype, but lead singer Peter Murphy said:

> It was a very tongue-in-cheek song which sounded extremely serious, very heavy-weight and quite dark. The mistake we made is that we performed it with naïve seriousness! That's what pushed the audience into it as a much more serious thing. The intense intention going into the performance actually overshadowed the humor of it. Because of that, the Gothic tag was always there.[9]

Hawkins's caricature is so cartoonish, so outrageous that it's hard to believe there could be any truth to it, but he claimed he really did practice voodoo. Director Jim Jarmusch cast Hawkins as the manager of a rundown hotel in his 1989 film *Mystery Train*. During the filming, production was halted due to relentless rain. Jarmusch relates in the documentary, *I Put a Spell on Me*:

> Jay took out all these bones he had in a little leather bag. He rolled them out on this table and said, "Alright, go set your cameras up because it's gonna stop raining." We said, "Come on Jay are you serious?" He said, "Well I'm half serious. Let's go see." And, like five minutes later it stopped raining and it didn't rain again the whole time we were shooting.

Regardless of whether or not he had any powers, I think he liked freaking white people out and must have gotten some satisfaction that they would give him money for the privilege. To put a finer point on it, in 1991 he released an album called *Black Music for White People.*

LeRoi Jones says that "each phase of the Negro's music issued directly from the dictates of his social and psychological environment," and nothing quite encapsulates the sound of the contemporary Black gothic as horrorcore, a subgenre of hip-hop in which the classic themes of racism, gang violence, drugs, police brutality, and poverty use the language of horror movies to tell their story. Hip-hop has always been a vehicle for telling stories about the Black urban experience, but horrorcore goes deeper and darker into the B-movie, slasher nightmare of psychosis, Satanism, cannibalism, mutilation, necrophilia, suicide, murder, and torture. The bands and their members have puny names like the Gravediggaz', Prince Paul (The Undertaker), Frukwan (The Gatekeeper), Poetic (The Grym Reaper) and RZA (The RZArector). Gravediggaz's album, *6 Feet Deep,* was released overseas as *Niggamorti*s. While the names might have a dark humor to them the lyrics and the stories they tell speak to the real condition of Black lives under centuries of white suppression and its psychological ramifications.[10]

In "Diary of a Madman," the Gravediggaz are in court, pleading insanity on a murder charge. The defense: the conditions of being a Black man in America, of surviving centuries of subjugation and inherited trauma and the attempt to thrive in a society that values you as a commodity but condemns you as a person is enough to drive a person insane. Living as a Black person is to exist in a state of madness and violence, which is not only inevitable, but it is a form of normalcy. RZArector raps:

> The year 84, November, day 10
> Overwhelmed by the wicked inspirations of an evil jinn
> I realize my ideas has spawned for 400 years
> Of blood sweat and tears

Detroit native, Esham The Unholy (Esham A. Smith), one of the founding fathers of horrorcore, raps about suicide in *American Psycho*, and the video depicts images of barren trees, skulls and dripping blood. He appears dressed in a suit and the title references the postmodern horror novel of vacuous corporate greed and rampant materialism in which serial killer, Patrick Bateman, has a meaningless job, unearned wealth, and a personality created by commodities. Esham's *American Psycho*, feels the business end of Bateman's capitalist agenda. Patrick Bateman is bottle service vodka and cocaine, Esham is a blunt dipped in PCP. While Bateman murders other people, Esham's psycho self-destructs.

Esham wrote the lyrics for his debut album *Boomin' Words from Hell* in 1988 when he was only thirteen and says:

> It was the crack era, when I made *Boomin'*, and that's where all that really came from. The city we lived in and just the turmoil that our city was going through at the time. We referred to the streets of Detroit as 'Hell' on that record. So that's where my ideas came from.[11]

Esham later dropped the "unholy" and horrorcore became acid rap. His music is now more about evoking positivity and less about violence and psychosis and in 2008 he even made a run for mayor of Detroit. But even in the desire to do social good ("People think I'm makin' this run for exposure, I'm tryin' to stop these homes from foreclosure.") there is still a wink and a nod to the darkness as he announced his candidacy with an EP called *Esham 4 Mayor*. In the song "First Day in Office" he raps:

I'm runnin' for the mayor and don't ask me why
Only thing you should do is just vote or DIE, DIE, DIE, DIE, DIE

When my Aunt Joan passed away the service was full of singing. She was a singer, her daughter is a singer and her friends were singers. I can't sing and when obliged to sing from a hymnal I spend much of the time just mouthing the words. I feel awkward in these moments, struggling to feel what everyone else seemed to feel singing "This Little Light of Mine", to believe what everyone else is believing. When family gathered before the service, eating and talking and catching up, I spotted a worn, brown book on the piano. It was her book of spirituals that she must have had for decades. The object resonated with me more than the songs themselves as I flipped through the pages, reading lyrics now and then, touching pages that absorbed decades of sounds and the voice of my family.

My Aunt Joan's song book, photo by L. Taylor

THE HOUSE ON BOSTON BOULEVARD

Not a house in the country ain't packed to its rafters with some dead Negro's grief.
— Toni Morrison, *Beloved*

Whenever there was a strange, unaccounted for noise in our house in Detroit, my dad would say, "It's just the house settling." No one ever explained to me what that meant, but the idea that something as stable as a house could be "unsettled" is… unsettling. It implies that the house is a bit uncomfortable, shifting in its seat trying to find the right spot, or that the house is disturbed, anxious, or unsatisfied with its lot. Built in 1924, our presence was merely one more chapter in its story, and as in all old houses, the previous pages showed through. The paint on the front door had been violently stripped, leaving it naked and raw in preparation for a fresh coat that would never come. Leaks and rainstorms meant strategically placed trashcans and buckets had been scattered around my room, and I slept with one eye open, waiting for them to spill over.

Like many old houses, ours had the architectural remnants of a lifestyle that no longer existed. There was a superfluous door in the hallway that served as a secret access to the staircase, a dumbwaiter I never had the courage to climb inside and a perpetually stuffy but spacious attic. We never used the backyard garage for some reason,

The Abbey in the Oakwood, *Caspar David Friedrich, 1809*

Detroit *photo by Sarah Feinstein*

and I would peek through the dusty, broken windows to stare at the old water-stained boxes inside, wondering what they were hiding: evidence of a murder or classified CIA documentation of aliens? Maybe a cursed doll harboring an evil spirit set on revenge? The only explanation I ever got was that it was so-called "paperwork" left behind by the previous owner. I didn't buy it.

In the summer, there were invasions of bats, daddy long-legs, and the occasional human. In our time there, our house was broken into five times, and in one particularly personal theft, burglars stole a box of rusty old tools that belonged to my grandfather, the pin my mother received when she graduated from nursing school, and the change from my piggy bank. The house was never entirely ours. The past was always present, and the outside was always creeping in.

If you started at my house walking east down my old street, past the Barry Gordy mansion, after about a mile you'd reach a one-hundred-year-old, two-story Tudor. During one particularly brutal Michigan winter in 2015, a pipe burst in the upper floors, flooding the house from the top to the basement, water cascading out of the windows and freezing into a massive solid waterfall. In effect, it turned the house into a giant popsicle, earning it the nickname, "The Boston Cooler," after a local treat of Vernors ginger ale and ice cream. The image is both shocking and beautiful. Each window is obscured and there are no photographs of the interior, so this bizarre spectacle is made even more mysterious by our being denied access to the heart of the chaos, but one can imagine pots and pans, armchairs, books, sweaters and table lamps frozen in space like bits of fruit floating in Jell-O. The house was purchased for $70,000 in 2011, but the owner was unable to keep up with the property taxes. So it was foreclosed, put up for auction, and padlocked without his knowledge, with all of his belongings still inside: furniture, tools, clothes, computers… It is an uncanny image; houses are not supposed to freeze into blocks of ice. The living room is not supposed to have thick, long icicles dripping down from the ceiling, the toilet is not supposed to be encased in ice. Nature and neglect turned what used to be a home into a sideshow attraction, a mutation of what security is supposed to look like. Obscure economic structures and environmental forces infiltrate spaces of comfort and stability, transforming a home into an object of terror like an eco-horror home invasion. My heart breaks for the owner, a pastor who lost everything he had, but I can't stop looking at the photos.

We know how the gothic dresses, its color, its sound and its sentiment, but if the gothic sensibility was an object it would be the extreme conspicuous futility of the ruin. Time and the elements create a specific kind of decay. It's not the decisive human design of vandalism or real-estate razing, but the relentless pull of physics and the chaos of the weather. The Livingstone House was a beautifully monstrous example of this. Neglect bent and twisted the building into organic forms, with shapes that are unpredictable and unfathomable, evoking a titillating slippage between the natural and the constructed that is both frightening and captivating.

Heavier on the left side, the house sags as if it has had a stroke, earning it the nickname "Slumpy." The rectangular

The Livingstone House (aka Old Slumpy), photo by Kim via Flickr,
August 2, 2007

window frames have shifted down into parallelograms. The conical roof of its three-story tower points slightly to the left instead of straight up. The left side, where the front door used to be, leans to the right, and the front facade has slipped off, revealing the first and second floors and exposing the pale green wall of an empty closet. It is a structure that by all rights should not exist in a modern city and it's a rare treat to witness a house of such stature age naturally — not torn down or lived-in but left to rot. It's no surprise that Slumpy was one of the most photographed ruined buildings in Detroit.

In 1894, William Livingstone, Jr, publisher of the *Detroit Evening Journal* and former president of the Dime Savings Bank, commissioned architect Albert Kahn to design his residence on Eliot Street in the posh neighborhood of Brush Park. Designed in the French Renaissance Revival style, the Livingstone House was a classic example of Detroit in the Gilded Age when the city was known as the "Paris of the Midwest." With the advent of the automobile in the early 1900s, people began moving further away from the city center, and single-family mansions were divided into apartments. As the auto industry boomed, freeways sliced through residential neighborhoods, leading people out of the city, but when the auto industry died, Brush Park went from being tony to derelict. The stately Victorian mansions that used to house society's elites became dilapidated, drooping ruins like monumental Miss Havishams.

Around 1987, the Red Cross purchased the land with the intent of demolishing the house to build a new headquarters, but preservationists intervened and succeeded in saving the house by moving the building one block east. Unfortunately, its new foundation was not strong enough to support it and thus began a twenty-year slide into decay. Too expensive to either rehabilitate or tear down, the Livingstone House was abandoned to sink under its own weight. The houses that used to be on either side had long been razed, leaving it abandoned and alone in its decline. Slumpy was eventually put out of its misery and torn down in the late 1990s.

The decayed and ruined house is a cornerstone of the Gothic landscape. The decrepit castle, neglected manor, or abandoned Victorian house with creaking doors, crumbling walls and dripping ceilings are classic ingredients of the horror aesthetic. From the ruins of Medieval abbeys scattered across the post-reformation English countryside, emerged a fascination with architectural decay that has ever since been fundamental to the Gothic topography. In the eighteenth century, the architectural folly was a homage to a romanticized Medieval past, and faux war-torn remnants of archways and crumbling castle walls became fashionable lawn decor for the aristocracy. Paintings like, *A Ruined Gothic Church beside a River by Moonlight*, by Sebastian Pether and *The Abbey in the Oakwood*, by Caspar David Friedrich, romanticized the ruin with misty melancholic nostalgia. In Ann Radcliffe's epic novel, *The Mysteries of Udolpho*, Emily observes that the castle's "mouldering walls of dark grey stone, rendered it a gloomy and sublime object…" In Edgar Allan Poe's, "The Fall of the House of Usher," the house's "principal feature seemed to be that of an excessive antiquity, the discoloration of ages had been great. Minute fungi overspread the whole exterior, hanging in a fine tangled web-work from the caves." The device has endured over the decades. The horror film, *Dark Water*, takes place in a dilapidated 1970s-era apartment building on Roosevelt Island in New York City. Originally known as Blackwell's in the nineteenth century, the island was home to a penitentiary, the New York City Lunatic Asylum, and the Small Pox hospital whose ruins are still there. In the film, an ominous leaky ceiling above a little girl's bed is enough to create a dreadful atmosphere, and the persistent, spotty black dampness that expands and grows elevates the ordinary annoyance of home maintenance to the horrific.

The ruin has no value other than as a spectacle, a metaphor representing our fear of the abandonment of civilization and our powerlessness over nature. The modern ruin speaks to both the pleasure and the anxiety of bearing witness to the limits of a post-industrial economy and the satisfaction of watching nature's comeuppance. The ruin exists in a temporal liminality "[permitting] the viewer to see the intact object and its disappearance at the same time."[1] Like a zombie, the ruin is both alive and dead. Like a ghost, the ruin is here, yet not.

The fascination with the decay of the constructed environment and the proliferation of "ruin porn" (photographs fetishizing urban blight) shifts the aesthetics of disrepair and abandonment from the visual language of economic decline and into the realm of romanticism and entertainment, and there is a bitter irony in the commodification of the devalued. In the television series *Abandoned* on Viceland, host Rick McCrank skateboards through a deserted shopping mall in Ohio, a former nuclear power plant in the Pacific northwest, a crumbling NASCAR racetrack in North Carolina, and of course through the streets of Detroit. He takes us on a tour of the usual suspects: the monumental Central Station, the vast and crumbling Packard Plant, and the once-glamorous Michigan Theater turned parking garage. The 2010s saw a surge of coffee-table books of beautifully photographed derelict spaces conspicuously void of people, like specimen books of urban waste. These photographs allow a voyeuristic view of the inaccessible: *The Ruins of Detroit* by Yves Marchand & Romain Meffre, *Detroit Disassembled* by Andrew Moore, and *Lost Detroit: Stories Behind the Motor*

City's Majestic Ruins by Dan Austin. There are images of a lawn of moss growing on the floor of an empty office, a school gymnasium with wooden floors so warped they look like rolling waves, and a knee-high pile of mugshots, wanted posters, and sheets of fingerprints in an old police station. In these frozen moments of ordinary life, the ephemeral becomes permanent and the permanent becomes ephemeral — and they are mesmerizing. I know the smell of exploitation, and that they ignore the people who live and work and play there, that they romanticize poverty and fetishize economic decay, but I keep looking. I shake my head at the piles of school books left to rot but I can't deny the thrill of seeing society crumble right before my very eyes.

Michigan autumns remain for me the platonic-ideal of the season, and neither Ohio or New York can live up to my memory of a north-east crispness in the air, fresh warm doughnuts and hot apple cider, and leaves that stayed vibrant reds, oranges, and yellows for months not weeks. And Detroit in the late Seventies and early Eighties was the ideal time and place for Halloween. I grew up in that sweet latch-key kid spot, so my parents were attentive enough to give our candy a quick pass for razor blades but relaxed enough to let me and my friends roam the moonlit streets by ourselves. Even on our relatively preserved neighborhood, there was the occasional spooky Victorian house with boarded-up windows painted black (ideal for a vampire lair) and overgrown abandoned lots with tall weeds that rustled inexplicably when we walked by. On 31 October the veil between the living and the dead was lifted, disbelief was suspended, and the night belonged to us kids.

The same cannot be said for the night before Halloween.

It wasn't until we left Michigan that I realized the night before Halloween, known as Devil's Night, was a phenomenon unique to Detroit. What started in the 1930s with innocent pranks and mischief (soaping car windows, egging houses, and toilet papering trees), by the 1970s had grown into a night of extreme vandalism and arson — it was a given that you didn't go out on Devil's Night. On Halloween the fear and the danger were benign and self-imposed, but fear on the night before was real. One of my friends was even picked up by the police for being out on Devil's Night after curfew. On 30 October 1984, when I was twelve years old, I watched the local news with fear and excitement as 810 fires were reported throughout the city, earning Detroit the distinction of being the arson capital of the world.[2] A staticky recording of the traffic from that night is nightmarish, a real *War of the Worlds*, as one fire engine after another announces their positions: ladder 1 and engine 5 in service, engine 11 in service, engine 32 in service, engine 41 and ladder 16 in service, engine 40 in service, engine 5 in service, engine 6 in service, engine 21 in service, ladder 8 and engine 29 in service... It took seventy-two hours to extinguish all of the fires.

On 25 October 1984, Mayor Coleman Young held a press conference with the deputy chiefs and commanders from the police and fire department, representatives of the unions and the board of education, to assure the public that one thousand volunteer police cadets and reserves, citizens and neighborhood watches would be assembled in preparation for the night ahead. The on-duty police force would be tripled and fire personnel would increase by 33%. If you didn't know what this press conference was about, it would be terrifying. One would think an alien invasion was coming, or a catastrophic natural disaster was eminent, until he says what the hopes of this effort will be — returning the night before Halloween to what it used to be, a night for kids to have some fun.

1984 is on record as being the worst Devil's Night in the city's history. But the Devil's Night ten years later saw three hundred fires. That night Tomika Wilson's one-year-old daughter died when her apartment building went up in flames:

> Some Detroit residents accused Mayor Dennis Archer of preparing inadequately for Devil's Night. "He wanted to downplay it," said Ernestine Gordon. "He called it 'Halloween Eve.' You can't do that. It's Devil's Night. You have to treat it like it's going to explode."

The debauched chaos of Devil's Night has steadily declined over the years and the night was rebranded Angel Night by troops of citizen watchdogs. But Detroit still has the most fires per capita than any other city in America. Between 2013 and 2015, more than ten thousand fires broke out in houses, apartments, businesses, churches, schools and other structures, claiming about one-hundred-and-twenty lives. In the film, *The Crow*, the resurrected Eric Draven is seeking revenge for the rape and murder of his girlfriend and himself on Devil's Night. The film ends with the line: "Buildings burn, people die, but real love is forever."

While the creation of the city is an authoritative, systematized, and logical project, the reduction of the city is chaotic, random, and left to the whim of human behavior, nature, and economics. Detroit was once the fifth largest city in the country. In the early 1900s, the burgeoning auto industry brought a great migration of southerners up north to work in Henry Ford's factory. The 1940s brought a second wave, primarily of Blacks escaping the segregation of Jim Crow laws. However, they were still met with systemic racism and prejudicial hiring and housing practices. In the summer of 1967, after decades of police brutality, one of the most destructive and deadly riots in American history broke out. During the Rebellion, as locals call it, more than two thousand five hundred buildings were destroyed.

While the Rebellion was a defining moment in the city's history, there is no single reason for the downturn of Detroit, but multiple: white flight, corrupt politicians, the economic downturn in the Seventies, and rising crime rates. But the biggest factor was the decline of the American auto industry. "The city began to fall apart the minute Henry Ford began to build it. The car made Detroit and the car unmade Detroit. Detroit was built in some ways to be disposable." The city has seen a relentless decline in population, from 1,800,000 in 1950 to 713,000 in 2010. As of 2016, the number was 672,795. Nearly one in three properties in Detroit are considered blighted (blight is defined as properties that are exposed to the elements, not structurally sound, in need of major repairs, have suffered fire damage, or have become dumping grounds), leaving behind a landscape peppered with empty lots and houses swallowed up by vegetation. Pastoral vistas appear where lines of sturdy middle-class homes once stood side-by-side. Houses that were once flanked by other houses are left abandoned, turning the neatly planned grid of the city into an irregularly gapped patchwork. Every erasure used to be a habitat, each with their own collection of knick-knacks, their own indelible crayon scribbles on the walls, their own holes in the roofs and doorknobs that need replacing, secret hiding places and treasures hidden under floor-boards. These rectangular vestiges, as Georges Perec says, "are in a sense monumental vacancies that define, without trying, the memory-traces of an abandoned set of futures."

Only Lovers Left Alive

If someone asked fourteen-year-old me what the perfect movie would be, I'd say Jim Jarmusch making a vampire movie set in Detroit, with Tilda Swinton in it (I saw Derek Jarman's *Caravaggio* in the theater at fourteen so I've been a fan of her for a while). In *Only Lovers Left Alive*, Adam, a reclusive melancholic vampire, lives in a large decrepit Queen Anne house in Brush Park. Like the Livingstone House, it is flanked by nothingness. The empty, overgrown lots and the bare spaces on either side are palpable absences, and there seems to be nothing across the street. It's not the things in the landscape that are ominous, it is the emptiness, the lack of things, the fact that there is a landscape here at all. The isolation of Adam's house is both ominous and vulnerable, a location abandoned by society. Instead of the treacherous road to Dracula's castle on a hill, Adam's house is just down the street, yet it is just as eerie.

The interior of Adam's home is rich and full. There are layers of patterned rugs and drapery in warm jewel tones, a well-worn sofa, and walls covered in photographs and paintings of philosophers, poets, and scientists. There are musical instruments and recording equipment in every corner. It is a well-lived-in space. By contrast, the exterior is barren, eerily isolated, and if not dead, it's certainly dying. Adam, who is contemplating suicide, is psychologically in sync with the diminishing spirit of the city. But having lived well beyond the scope of a human lifespan, he experiences the world on a scale closer to geological than anthropological. Adam's depression stems from the "zombies" (what he calls human beings) and our blatant disregard for the Earth. The film is peppered with references to climate change. While the Livingstone House seems at the mercy of the elements, in *Only Lovers Left Alive*, it is us people who are wrecking the joint.

Adam takes Eve (his partner of eons) on a tour of the city, and she notes, "So this is your wilderness. Detroit." They go past the deserted Packard Plant and the Michigan Theater, a majestic, French Renaissance showplace now used as a parking garage. Hitsville USA, the birthplace of Motown, isn't so interesting at night, but they do drive by Jack White's house. The streets are barren and dimly lit as if every other light on the block had been knocked out, a detail that is unfortunately accurate. In 2012, without the budget to repair eighty-eight thousand broken streetlights, the city proposed to reduce the number to forty-six thousand, plunging already crime-ridden and impoverished neighborhoods into darkness. In the film, everything is always hidden in the shadows and it seems to be perpetually three o'clock in the morning. There are never any pedestrians or cars on the streets and the only sounds are the occasional howl of some mysterious creature of the night in concert with a distant police siren.

It Follows

While the city has become a ready-made *mise-en-scene* for horror movies, *It Follows*, directed by David Robert Mitchell, takes place in the suburbs. As much as I would like to say that I am from Detroit, full stop, I can't. I was born in Cincinnati, Ohio, then after a year we moved to Amherst, Massachusetts, and from there to Michigan. When I tell people the long answer to the question "where are you from?" I go directly from Amherst to Detroit, skipping over Southfield, the suburb just outside of the city where we lived for two years. I remember little of that time, only that there was an eerie, flat, beigeness to the place. When I picture it now I see vast office parks and a subdivision with a perpetually empty playground. I remember being in a circle of other kids looking down at a dead bird, someone poking it with a stick. I remember a kid getting hit in the head with a baseball bat and the trail of blood down the school hallway as the gym teacher carried him away. I remember there was a girl I wanted desperately to be friends with, but I wouldn't go to her house because I was afraid of her dog (I assumed it was racist). While Detroit has arson, store clerks hidden behind bullet-proof glass, and hookers on the corner, it never creeped me out like Southfield did.

Filmmakers routinely use the suburbs as a location for horror — *Nightmare on Elm Street*, *Halloween*, *Poltergeist*, *Paranormal Activity*. The invasion of the monstrous becomes even more terrifying against the background of perceived security. Detroit, "an overwhelmingly black city [is framed as] the 'dark other,' a city to be isolated, feared, and cut off from the body of the nation."[3]

In *It Follows*, Jamie is the victim of a sexually trans-mitted curse in the form of a relentless, silent, shape-shifting entity. Jamie and her friends live in a middle-class, white, neighborhood and as her story begins, we see a chalk hopscotch grid on the sidewalk, a man mowing his lawn, and a handsome teenager washing his car. It's not a wealthy neighborhood, but it is comfortably normal. The time-frame is ambiguous. The decor of Jamie's house seems to be from the Seventies or Eighties, yet her friend reads a book from some electronic device not yet invented. For her date with Hugh, the couple go to a silent movie accompanied by an organ.

The scene in which Jamie becomes infected with the curse was shot in the parking lot of the abandoned Northville Psychiatric Hospital, a massive, oppressive building. The area is desolate and dark, except for a streetlamp spotlighting their car. Northville opened in 1952 but fell victim to the recession in the Seventies, resulting in significant overcrowding and neglected patients. The hospital eventually closed in 2003, becoming a popular destination for intrepid ghost hunters. The forest surrounding the hospital is known as the "Evil Woods."

After they have sex, Hugh knocks her out and ties her to a wheelchair, forcing her to witness the creature that will now be pursuing her. This scene is shot inside the abandoned Packard Plant. It's a vast and empty space of crumbling concrete and exposed rebar. The windows have long been broken out and the border between the inside and out is blurred. The Packard Plant opened in 1903, and at the time was considered the most modern automobile manufacturing factory in the world. Its forty-three-acre campus closed in 1956, and it is now known as the largest abandoned building in the world. Jamie and Hugh's relationship begins in a charming movie theater on a suburban main street. The attack occurs in the desolation of a failed state institution and an industrial wasteland.

Throughout the film, there is a contrast between the monster's spaces and the victim's spaces. If Jamie doesn't pass the curse on by having sex with someone else, the entity will kill her and resume its pursuit of Hugh. He leaves the safety of the suburbs and flees into the city, hiding out in a decrepit abandoned house, one of many such houses on his street. Jamie and her friends decide to find Hugh, and as they drive into the city, they pass row after row of boarded-up shops, run-down houses and empty lots.

In *Only Lovers Left Alive*, Adam and Eve's drive through Detroit is portrayed with philosophical contemplation and historical perspective, much like tourists visiting the ruins of Ancient Rome. In *It Follows*, the trip into the city is depicted as a dangerous journey, marked with dread. As the group marches back into the city to kill the entity, it is with defiant gravitas and the atmosphere of an epic quest. Unlike their suburb, the people on the street are all Black. The city represents "unplanned obsolescence, crime, and, of course, unchecked blackness," and euphemisms like "inner city" and "urban" are known codes for African American. As they walk past boarded-up houses and into a distinctly impoverished Black neighborhood, one character says:

> When I was a little girl my parents never let me go south of 8 Mile and I never knew what that meant until I got a little older and I realized that's where the city started and the suburbs ended.

In stalking its prey, the entity follows Jamie and her friends into their territory — their neighborhood, their homes, and their school — but the dirty work of disposing of the monster happens in Detroit. *It Follows* is a "not in my backyard" battle framed as a horror story.

The sublimity of the modern ruin lies in its relative newness, the purpose and life of the former building are familiar and recognizable, creating the dichotomy between the attraction and repulsion of our world gone to dust. We see ourselves in a state of decay. We are watching our own death and in the photographs, ruin-porn websites, documentaries, and horror movies we become mourners at our own funeral. There is dark pleasure in this glimpse of the end of civilization, a taste of life after the apocalypse. Eugene Thacker calls this nebulous zone the "world-with-out-us." It is a glimpse at what our world would be like without people, a place in which human beings are inconsequential. It's not that nature doesn't care about us, or is purposely exhibiting its domination. The world doesn't even know we're here. In ruined spaces, nature, the original master builder, takes over, defying gravity and eschewing structural integrity, reminding us of what we once were and how small we really are.

I have an uneasy relationship with ruin porn. There is a guilty pleasure in these images (hence the "porn" connotation), but having grown up in Detroit, it's uncomfortable seeing my hometown perceived as sociological experiment, an art project, or a bargain-basement real-estate deal. There is a dissonance between my fascination with these images and the circumstances of their making. The ability to delight in the ruin is a privileged position. The spectacle of annihilation is only pleasurable when you're not the one being annihilated and the aesthetics of decay can fall into the trap of romanticizing poverty. It's easy to gape at the remains, but these images are the result of economic decline, political corruption, systemic racism, violence, and apathy.

In *Only Lovers Left Alive*, Adam and Eve drive past the Fox Theater (where I saw the Smiths), and in the film, it looks ominous and desolate. But the Fox Theater has since been renovated and is now absolutely glorious. Eve sees the desolation of the city as an interesting moment in the life of a place, just another sliver along the spectrum of time.

She tells Adam, "This place will rise again. There's water here. When the cities in the south are burning, this place will bloom." As of January 2017, eighty-eight thousand dead streetlights were replaced with sixty-five thousand brand new LED lights. Brush Park, where Slumpy once stood and where Adam the vampire made his home, is currently undergoing a massive redevelopment, filling in the awkward gaps of abandoned lots with restaurants, shops, and sustainable LEED certified houses. In 2018, Detroit was voted "one of the hottest cities to visit" by the travel guide, *Lonely Planet*. Anthony Bourdain filmed an episode of "Parts Unknown" there, and the home of Adam the vampire was, for a while, available to rent as an Airbnb.

If southern gothic was about Postbellum America, Detroit certainly represents a post-Industrial American gothic. It is a revenant city — its motto is "*Speramus Meliora; Resurget Cineribus:*" "We hope for better days; it shall rise from the ashes" — burning and rising from the flames over and over and over again.

FEAR OF A BLACK
PLANET

*I am an invisible man. No, I am not a spook like those who
haunted Edgar Allan Poe: nor am I one of your Hollywood-
movie ectoplasms. I am a man of substance, of flesh and bone,
fiber and liquids — and I might even be said to possess a
mind. I am invisible, understand, simply because people
refuse to see me.*
— Ralph Ellison, *Invisible Man*

we are deathlessness
awakening
from a deep deep sleep
— M. Lamar, *Funeral Doom Spiritual*

The assumption that goths are categorically depressed
misanthropes has always bothered me. It's a lazy judgment
based on a very narrow definition of what happiness is
supposed to look like. When this occurs I point people to
Morticia and Gomez Addams, one of the most blissfully
romantic couples in popular culture. It's for these same
reasons why we don't consider the blues a morbid or bleak
form of music. It's a glorification of sentiment.

It may use horror, death, melancholy, and the macabre
in its methodology, but the gothic (and goth) is above
all else romanticism. Both the gothic and the romantic
have the issue of being nebulous things to define, but

they both "privilege the imagination" over reason, and resist bourgeois social norms for what is internal and emotional.[1] The Gothic is an anathema to order and rationality, forgoing restraint for excess. It will always choose the fanciful over the pragmatic, the numinous over the tangible. It is a black-velvet-in-the-summer kind of culture and if you are Black, to willingly succumb to a life of whimsey is foolish at the least and dangerous at the worst. Colonialism comes with vigilance (both from the colonists and the colonizers), with the exhausting strain of disaster preparedness, and this frivolous pursuit is a belly exposing vulnerability.

The Privilege of Frivolity

A video circling around my social media feeds show a group of goth guys in front of a nondescript office building. Dressed in long black skirts, black zippered pants, and black t-shirts, they stand out against the drab grey/beige building, chosen perhaps for its strikingly paradoxical blandness. There's no sound, but from the frenetic yet precise dance moves and the outfits, they resemble a post-apocalyptic cheerleading team, and I can guess that the genre of music they're dancing to is industrial. They are an unabashedly misfit collective, taking their fun seriously.

Expertly Photoshopped into the foreground is a Black boy, around eight or nine years old, in a yellow t-shirt, creating a stark contrast to the white skin and black clothes behind him. He's standing stock still, holding a beverage and staring straight ahead. Then with perfect comedic timing, his eyes shift toward the camera with a deadpan look that can best be described as WTF — what Margo Jefferson calls the "survival side eye."

This phenomenon is known as "digital blackface." There is a library online of snippets of videos capturing a smug smirk and eyeroll plucked from television shows, movies or personal videos to be copied and pasted when words fail or are too cruel for language. The fed-up Black woman smirking as she grabs her purse to go, the old Black woman fainting in church overcome with the spirit, the dramatic sassy entrance of a reality TV show contestant; they are all removed from context to become human emojis symbolizing disgust, excitement, or confidence. The affective currency of Black people is traded back and forth all day on Twitter, Tumblr and Facebook.

I get it. I give the video a digital thumbs up and respond with an unenthusiastic LOL, but like most memes, the joke is usually at someone else's expense, and by the third or fourth time someone sent it to me, it stopped being funny. The Black kid in the yellow shirt represents the straight man, the seasoned foil to this spooky suburban weirdness. The punch-line relies on a construct of Blackness, in which there is an expectation of gravitas and wisdom, and a burden of cool. Goth lies in that realm of "crazy shit white people do," along with Burning Man and Renaissance Fairs and things that are ostentatiously frivolous — attributes contradictory to the Black veneer of skepticism and street savvy. This "coolness coat of arms" is a clever way of avoiding vulnerability by using a bulwark of dignity to protect oneself from the danger of racism. It also strips away authenticity, subjectivity, and play, leaving little room for velvet top-hats and black-lace parasols.

In the video, the dancers do not acknowledge the kid because he was never there. The kid never saw those goth dancers. He wasn't passing judgment on anyone. Someone clipped him out and expertly edited him in, using him to judge by proxy, speaking for everyone who thought they were lame or ridiculous or geeky but were too afraid to say so. His presence is not just saying, "Look at these weirdos," it's saying, "Look at these white folks," with a confounded shake of the head. What bothered me the most about the use of the judgmental Black kid in the video is that it falls into that tired old gag of "white folks do this / black folks to that" mentality, and puts the clothes, the music, the dancing into another category of things Black people don't do.

In the original video, the boy is standing in line at a fast-food restaurant. Next to him is a little girl and his shifting glance reads more like the nervous confusion of a first crush. It's a boring moment in comparison. In the original he is not representing anything but himself, just pudgy sweetness, but when re-purposed in the other context, he is superior coolness.

Ta-Nehisi Coates' book *Between the World and Me* is a letter to his son, warning him about the world he's been born into, in which he is made suspect just by existing. He warns his son about the dangers of falling for the "American Dream," a promise that was never intended for him, which as a Black man can be a distracting and disarming pipe dream, a dangling carrot. He says:

> As a black man I could not afford the luxury of dreams, of lighter thoughts. A third of my attention span was devoted towards survival. I think I somehow knew that

that third of my brain should have been concerned with more beautiful things.

He writes about the constant vigilance against saying the wrong thing in the wrong place, of walking down the wrong street at the wrong time, and the persistent mistrust of the world he lived in and the people who ran it.

The goth dancers are free to use that extra third of their brain for "beautiful" things, and can enjoy the luxury of self-determined otherness. The gothic encourages a slowness prone to daydreaming and longing for something other than the here and now. It is a culture whose mind is elsewhere, a dangerous attribute for a Black person in America, where meandering or lingering is considered a threat worthy of deadly force, and where simply existing in a space is enough to warrant a call to the police. Being Black in America comes with a baseline of anxiety, a consistent fight-or-flight response that is calmed from time to time, but ready at any moment — and it is exhausting.

In the midst of the Black Lives Matter movement, the hashtag #CarefreeBlackKids2k16 began making the rounds as a balm to counteract the barrage of images online of dead Black bodies on sidewalks and weeping mothers. According to Monica Williams, clinical psychologist and director of the Center for Mental Health Disparities at the University of Louisville, "graphic videos (vicarious trauma) combined with lived experiences of racism, can create severe psychological problems reminiscent of post-traumatic stress syndrome." Articles extolling the "carefree black man" appeared and little girls exuded Black Girl Magic. Photographer Andre L. Perry published a book called *Happy Black People: Vol.1* (it's refreshing to assume there will be a volume two). Tropes like The Stoic Blackman and The Thug, The Angry Black Woman or The All-Knowing Magical Negro are so pervasively insidious that public acts of authentic happiness and embarrassing silliness become a kind of dissent. In the effort to humanize the victims of police violence, the instinct is to show mothers clutching framed school photographs, to Say Their Names. But it can have the opposite effect in creating another symbol, another icon — the Grieving Black Mother. But in the same way that stoicism and mourning can be an act of protest, so can flagrant absurdity.

Coates called it "the luxury of dreams — of lighter thoughts." To take one's eyes off the prize for just a minute can be misconstrued as a reckless naivety, but the lighter (or darker) thoughts are the best kind. In the season finale of the HBO series *Random Acts of Flyness*, a Black woman whispers into the void, "You are entitled to flaw, folly, fuck ups, failure, foolishness, fuckery, phantasm, fixation […] without any harm coming to your person, spirit, or earning potential." A reminder that frivolity is a right that must be taken and insisted upon, and I quite like this militant stance in defense of humanism, the right to fantasy and a future.

It's why I understand the desire and the need for a Black Panther perception of the world, one in which history can be reimagined, and reclaimed, a history in which the transatlantic slave trade never happened. What would it look like if colonialism never happened? AfroFuturism takes a technocultural perspective of the African diaspora and reimagines a world not framed by white supremacy, and instead envisions a universe that orbits around Blackness.

While futurism may seem the very opposite of the gothic, they are both romanticized views of the past — one glorifies and the other corrects. It is a decisively non-white historical reconstruction of a "lost future," a nostalgia for what should have been.[2] It may seem contradictory, but there is an optimism to the AfroGothic in its reclamation of history.

I saw M. Lamar before I heard his music and felt that little burst of warm familiarity when seeing a fellow brown-skinned punk rock/goth/metal person — the other one in the room. His eyes are heavily ringed with black and a bandanna holds back long, mussed, straight black hair. He is rail thin with tight black pants in the classic goth balance of feminine and masculine. He wears a gigantic inverted cross necklace and heavy silver rings on every finger. He hits all the right notes in the visual language of goth, so much so that it is at first a bit surprising to hear his music, but after one moment it's not surprising at all.

Badass Nigga, digital video still, 2014, Directed by M. Lamar, Cinematography by Ned Stresen-Reuter

Musician/artist M. Lamar is a self-described "NEGRO-GOTHIC devil-worshiping free black man in the blues tradition," who sings in an operatic counter-tenor, channeling Leontyne Price, coupled with wailing howls like Diamanda Galás, pulling from negro spirituals and field songs. Composer and collaborator Hunter Hunt-Hendrix describes M. Lamar as "a queer goth opera singer of field spirituals." Lamar work lies "between the Eighties counter-cultural aesthetic and Faulknerian South there is a paradoxical ligament, a wormhole between worlds flashing as a psychotic horizon for them both."

M. Lamar is not subtle, but dramatic, operatic, melancholic, and unapologetically Black and gothic. In the video for "Badass Nigga (Charlie Looker Remix)," he sits elegantly next to a pillory, drinking a glass of wine and reading a copy of *Beloved*. In "Legacies," he ascends gallows in a long, hooded black robe. He's holding a black leather bullwhip to his waist and there are three white shirtless young men kneeling at his feet. Superimposed over the images is an inverted cross, inside of which is an illustration of a lynching. A hooded white man then guillotines the bullwhip, leaving the castrated tail to drop in a basket below while M. Lamar sings in a soaring soprano: "He cut off my father's private part and likes to play with mine." In "Trying to Leave My Body," he sings of human cargo "in the belly of the ship," standing on a stool, leaning towards a noose, his hands reaching out and mouth open in a kind of catatonic rigor.

M. Lamar is a study in restrained excess; the uncanny occupation of multiple eras, multiple genres, multiple voices and multiple genders is both thrilling and disquieting. We aren't sure what we are looking at or who we are listening to. You can't separate M. Lamar's physical presence from his voice. The voice alone would be a ghostly nostalgia, the operatic trill and the death metal howl, the sounds of layers of anguish through the ages, on top of each other as an aural palimpsest. It is spectral, but a specter we recognize. When I saw M. Lamar, the clothes, the eyeliner, a ring on each finger, I was yanked into the now (or the near-now), and there was a new context to those ghosts, one that was from *my* past as well as from my ancestors'.

Make America Goth Again

Gothic Lamb is a Black-owned goth clothing brand. The tagline on their Instagram says "Depressed, Stressed, & Black Obsessed," a slogan that could apply to the African American experience or to a moody emo kid. Among the shirts with slogans like "Future Corpse" and beanies emblazoned with "666" is a black baseball hat with the phrase "Make America Goth Again" a re-imagining of Donald Trump's infamous catch phrase, "Make America Great Again." It begs the question, when was America great before? The insistence of the cis-het, white, suburban middle-class or rural working-class, as an idyllic representation of America, has always been an illusion. It is less about *when* America was great, but *for whom* it was great. The role of the gothic is to pull back the curtains on the idyllic and show the dark, the mystery, and the reality, and that includes the fallacy of the one-true American. There is no greater crime to goth than tedium and the homogenous drive for conspicuous mediocrity is just boring.

The first horror movie I ever saw was *Invasion of the Body Snatchers* in the theater in 1978 when I was six years old. I was with my older brother, who I assume would have preferred not to have to babysit me. Imprinted in my mind is Donald Sutherland's gaping mouth and wide eyes pointing accusingly at the real humans with an alien screech. It was clear that the replicant pod people would be taking over, that there were only a few human survivors left, and that the only way to resist replication was to stay awake. Aside from the trauma of seeing a human head on a tiny dog, I wonder if deep in my mind something had been imprinted — to never be a pod person, to run away at all costs and remain human... and to stay awake.

I am anticipating that one-true goths will disagree with me; that cultural purists will say that goth(ic) is British and white, hands down; that music critics will complain that I haven't mentioned Christian Death, Fields of the Nephilim, or Militia Vox; that gate-keepers will question my credibility. But just as there is no one-true American, there is no one-true goth. In all its variation of fashion and music, its essence is an ineffable sublimity, and the harder you try to solidify it, the more liquid it gets. But it can be distilled to one common point, the axiom by which all goths and the gothic is understood: **Black**.

My favorite genre of horror is the haunted house, and of this sub-genre *Poltergeist* is my number one. Unlike the castle in *The Castle of Otranto*, the Poltergeist house wasn't a moldering manor on a hill taken over by vines. It is a new construction in a subdivision, one that expands and grows in an ominous "sprawl." The evil that threatens the Freeling family goes to the heart of the American promise: home ownership.

Steven Freeling is the top salesman for the Cuesta Verde planned community in southern California, distributing the American dream through sunken living rooms and wall-to-wall carpeting. Unfortunately, his Phase One house has sucked his daughter into some alternate metaphysical dimension, originating in the children's bedroom closet. He discovers that not only was the house built on top of a cemetery, but that they only moved the headstones and left the bodies. From a hill looking down upon the tidy rows of the idyllic Cuesta Verde planned community, behind them is a dismal view of old neglected tombstones, resembling something you'd see in the Old Country, not Orange County. His boss, Mr Teague, explains his plans to expand Cuesta Verde on to the cemetery land, that the graves and markers would be moved to another cemetery nearby. Freeling, is doubtful, but says with trepidation:

Freeling: *I suppose that'd be okay.*
Teague: *For who?*
Freeling: *For whoever might complain.*
Teague looks at him quizzically: *No one's complained until now.*

America has always been goth — from field hollers to the Sunken Place, the role of the Black gothic has served as the shadow over the shining city on the hill. The Black gothic rips the mask off of the thief and the villain who would have gotten away with it if it wasn't for those meddling kids. Every time the veil is lifted, when the zombies get woke, when the skeletons come out of the closet, when the ghosts start complaining, is when America gets goth.

The first track on M. Lamar's *Funeral Doom Spiritual,* "The Demon Rising," is a prolonged guttural wavering growl and an occasional high-pitched cry under a thunderous piano trill and the consistent boom of a bass drum. It reminds me of Stravinsky's "The Rite of Spring," a disorienting, primal, fearsome piece, suggesting something large being awoken from a long hibernation. Or as M. Lamar puts it, "a Negro zombie apocalypse":

> The dead can't sing, but we know that the dead are singing to us all the time through spirituals and black music. If the dead can't sing then maybe they're just asleep. And if they're sleeping there's always the possibility of awakening.

Unlike the mindless gait of the risen dead, this zombie is charged, activated —the waking of a sleeping giant. This awakening, this state of "woke," shows itself in resistance, resting in power instead of peace. The dead still have work to do. This is what the gothic does, it does the work of processing our darkest fears, molding our deepest trauma into something not just manageable, but pleasurable. While everyone is asleep the gothic is up in the middle of the night making beautiful music.

In the 2016 British horror film, *The Girl with all the Gifts*, directed by Colm McCarthy, Melanie (Sennia Nanua) is a Black girl of about ten years old with a neat TWA (Teenie Weenie Afro) and an eager-to-please smile.[3] She sits in a concrete cell patiently waiting for armed military guards to strap her to a wheelchair. She greets them with polite "good mornings," addressing them each by name with the enthusiasm of a teacher's pet. In this post-apocalyptic world, the planet has been afflicted with a fungal infection that turns human beings into flesh-eating zombies. In a gruesome twist, for women who were pregnant at the time, the virus spread *invitro* and the zombified babies ate their way out of the womb, born with the incessant hunger for human flesh. Melanie is one of several such children, but is particularly charming and more human "presenting" than the rest. But her cleverness is dismissed as the virus mimicking human behavior. To them she is still monstrous, dangerous, and frightening. She eventually proves her specialness to the guards and scientists and warms them over, but when it becomes evident that the virus was winning and the zombies would rapidly outnumber them, one of her human allies bemoans that the world is over. She watches him die as the fungus takes over his body and says comfortingly: "It's not over, it's just not yours anymore."

BIBLIOGRAPHY

Adams, Julia and Steinmetz, George. *The Ruins of Modernity*. Durham: Duke University Press, 2010.

Apel, Dora. *Beautiful Terrible Ruins: Detroit and the Anxiety of Decline*. New Brunswick: Rutgers University Press, 2015.

Apel, Dora. "The Ruins of Capitalism." *Jacobin Magazine*, June 5, 2015.

Ahmed, Sara. *The Cultural Politics of Emotion*. "The Affective Politics of Fear." Routledge, 2015.

American Experience: The Murder of Emmett Till, PBS, 2003.

Barthes, Roland. *Mourning Diary*. New York: Hill and Wang, 2009.

Badiou, Alain. *Black: The Brilliance of a Non-Color*. Cambridge: Polity Press, 2016.

Binelli, Mark. "How Detroit Became the World Capital of Staring at Abandoned Old Buildings." *New York Times Magazine*. November 12, 2012.

Bogira, Steve. "They Came in Through the Bathroom Mirror: A Murder in the Projects." *Chicago Reader*, September 7, 1987.

Botting, Fred. *Gothic: The New Critical Idiom*. London: Routledge, 2014.

Bouie, Jamelle, and Jamelle Bouie. "'Fear' Was a Viable Defense for Killing Philando Castile. With Police and Black Victims, It Always Is." *Slate Magazine*, June 23, 2017. "Michael Brown Wasn't a Superhuman Demon to Anyone but Darren Wilson." *Slate Magazine*, November 26, 2014.

Bowley, Graham. "How the Fight for a National African-American Museum Was Won." *The New York Times*, September 4, 2016

Bradley, Regina N. "Getting in Line: Working Through Beyonce's 'Formation.'" *Red Clay Scholar*, Febuary 17, 2016, redclayscholarblog.

Brown, Vincent. *The Reaper's Garden: Death and Power in the World of Atlantic Slavery*. Cambridge: Harvard University Press, 2010.

Burke, Edmund. *A Philosophical Enquiry into the Sublime and the Beautiful*. London: Penguin Books, 2004.

Burton, Richard. *The Anatomy of Melancholy*. New York: New York Review Books, 2001.

Chafets, Ze'ev. "The Tragedy of Detroit." *New York Times Magazine*, July 29, 1990.

Chappelle's Show, S. 3 E.3, Writs. Neal Brennan (creator), Dir: Rusty Cundieff, Marobru Inc., 2006

CNN.com. "Police find icon's casket, more empty plots at historic cemetery." *Indianapolis Reporter*. July 10, 2009.

Coates, Ta-Nehisi. *Between the World and Me*. New York: Spiegel & Grau, 2015.

Cooper, Martha & Sciorra, Joseph. *RIP: Memorial Wall Art*. London: Thames & Hudson, 1994.

Cotter, Holland. "Review: The Smithsonian African American Museum Is Here at Last. And It Uplifts and Upsets." *The New York Times*, September 15, 2016.

Crabb, David. *Bad Kid: A Memoir*. New York: Harper Perennial, 2015.

Cundieff, Rusty. *Tales from the Hood*. 40 Acres & A Mule Filmworks, 1995.

Cunningham, Vinson. "Making a Home for Black History."

The New Yorker, August 29, 2016.

Davenport-Hines, Richard. *Gothic: Four Hundred Years of Excess, Horror, Evil and Ruin*. New York: North Point Press, 1998.

Davey, Monica and Ruethling, Gretchen. "After 50 Years, Emmett Till's Body is Exhumed." *The New York Times*, June 2, 2005.

Davison, Margaret Carol. *The Gothic and Death*. Manchester University Press, 2017.

Delgado, Melvin. *Death at an Early Age and the Urban Scene: The Case for Memorial Murals and Community Healing*. Westport: Praeger Publishers, 2003.

Delgado, Richard, and Jean Stefancic, eds. *Critical White Studies*. Toni Morrison, "Playing in the Dark: Whiteness and the Literary Imagination," Temple University Press, 1997, p. 79-81.

Douglass, Frederick. *Narrative of the Life of Frederick Douglass, an American Slave*. Penguin Books, 1994

Dickey, Colin. *Ghostland: An American History in Haunted Places*. New York: Viking, 2016.

Du Bois, W.E.B. *The Souls of Black Folk*. New York: Gramercy Press, 1994.

Dunlap, David W. "Evidence of Burial Ground Is Discovered in East Harlem." *New York Times*, January 21, 2016.

Ellison, Ralph. *Invisible Man*. New York: Vintage International, 1995.

Fiedler, Leslie A. *Love and Death in the American Novel*. Champaign: Dalkey Archive Press, 1997.

Ferber, Michael. *Romanticism: A Very Short History*. Oxford University Press, 2010.

Fisher, Mark. *Ghosts of My Life Writings on Depression,*

Hauntology and Lost Futures. Winchester: Zero Books, 2014.

Fisher, Mark. "For Your Unpleasure: The Hauteur-Couture of Goth." *k-punk, k-punk.abstractdynamics.org*, June 1, 205.

Fredrickson, George M. *Racism: A Short History*. Princeton: Princeton University Press, 2002.

Freud, Sigmund. *On Murder, Mourning and Melancholia*. New York: Penguin Books, 2004.

Fry, Gladys-Marie. *Night Riders in Black History*. Chapel Hill: The University of North Carolina Press, 1975.

Gordon, Avery F., and Janice Radway. *Ghostly Matters: Haunting and the Sociological Imagination*. Minneapolis: University of Minnesota Press, 1997.

"Diary of a Madman," Anthony Ian Berkeley, Arnold E. Hamilton, David Collins, Paul E. Huston, Robert F. Diggs, Walter Reed. Universal Music Publishing Group, 1994.

Groom, Nick. *The Gothic: A Very Short Introduction*. Oxford University Press, 2012.

Gunn, Bill, dir. *Ganja & Hess*, Kelly/Jordan Enterprises, 1973.

Halperin, Moze. "The Curious History of 'I Put a Spell on You.'" *Flavorwire*, February 12, 2015.

Harriman, Andi. *Some Wear Leather, Some Wear Lace: The Worldwide Compendium of Postpunk and Goth in the 1980s*. United Kingdom: Intellect Ltd., 2014.

Harris, Andrew and Pettersson, Edvard. "Ferguson Officer Darren Wilson Told Grand Jury He Feared for His Life" *Bloomberg.com*, Bloomberg, November 25, 2014.

Hartman, Saidiya V. *Scenes of Subjection: Terror, Slavery, and Self-Making in Nineteenth-Century America*. Oxford University Press, 2010, p. 33.

Hebdige, Dick. *Subculture: The Meaning of Style*. London: Routledge, 1979.

Hogle, Jerrold E. *The Cambridge Companion to Gothic Fiction*. Cambridge University Press, 2002.

Hopper, Toby, dir. *Poltergeist*. MGM, 1982.

Hopper, Toby, dir. *The Texas Chainsaw Massacre*. Vortex, 1974.

Huyssen, Andreas. "Present Pasts: Media, Politics, Amnesia." *Public Culture* 1 January 2000, p. 21–38.

Huyssen, Andreas. *Present Pasts, Urban Palimpsests and the Politics of Memory*. Stanford University Press, 2003, p. 28-29.

Kennedy, J. Gerald and Weissberg, Lianne. ed. *Romancing the Shadow: Poe and Race*. Oxford University Press, 2001.

Laqueur, Thomas W. *The Work of the Dead: a Cultural History of Mortal Remains*. Princeton: Princeton University Press, 2015.

Jackson, John L. Jr., *Real Black: Adventures in Racial Sincerity*. University of Chicago Press, 2005.

Jackson, Lauren Michele. "We Need to Talk About Digital Blackface in Reaction GIFs." *teenvogue.com*, August 2, 2017.

Jackson, Stanley W. *Melancholia and Depression*. New Haven: Yale University Press, 1986.

Jarmusch, Jim dir. *Only Lovers Left Alive*. Recorded Picture Company (RPC), 2013.

Jefferson, Margo. *Negroland*. New York: Pantheon Books, 2015.

Jefferson, Thomas. *Notes on the State of Virginia*, 1785.

Jenkins, Candice M. "African American Review." *African American Review*, vol. 38, no. 2, 2004, p. 344–345.

"Juneteenth," *Atlanta*, writ. Stefani Robinson and Donald

Glover, dir. Janicza Bravo. FX Productions, 2016.

Kant, Immanuel. "Analytic of the Sublime." *Critique of Judgement*. Oxford University Press, 2008.

Kennedy J., Gerald & Weissberg, Liliane. *Romancing the Shadow*. Oxford University Press, 2001.

M. Lamar, *Funeral Doom Spiritual*. RITA Books, 2016.

Lee, Spike, dir. *School Daze*. Columbia Pictures. 40 Acres & A Mule Filmworks, 1988.

Lewis, Matthew. *The Monk*. Oxford University Press, 2008. Marchand, Yves and Romain Meffre. *The Ruins of Detroit*. Germany: Steidl, 2010.

Margolick, David. *Strange Fruit: Biography of a Song*. New York: Harper Collins, 2001.

McCann, Ian. "I Put a Spell on You brought bliss to all who touched it — except its composer." *Financial Times*, February 6, 2017.

McCarthy, Colm dir. *The Girl with All the Gifts*. Poison Chef, 2016.

McKillop, Alan D. "Mrs. Radcliffe on the Supernatural in Poetry." *The Journal of English and Germanic Philology*, vol. 31, no. 3, 1932, p. 352–359.

Menato, Sara. "Saint Cecilia in V&A Collections." *V&A Blog*, July 11, 2016.

Robert Mitchell, David dir. *It Follows*. Northern Lights Films, 2014.

Morrison, Toni. *Beloved*. New York: Vintage International, 2004.

Morrison, Toni. "Playing in the Dark: Whiteness and the Literary Imagination." Richard Delgado and Jean Stefancic, ed. *Critical White Studies*, Temple University Press, 1997.

Moten, Fred. *In the Break: The Aesthetics of the Black Radical Tradition*. Minneapolis: University of Minnesota Press, 2003, p. 70.

Nance, Terrance, dir. *Random Acts of Flyness*. HBO, 2018.

Neal, Larry. "The Ethos of The Blues." *The Black Scholar* 3, no. 10, 1972, p. 42-48.

Norwood, Hermond. "Interview with Fountain Hughes, Baltimore, Maryland." Library of Congress. Baltimore, Maryland, November 6, 1949.

Nora, Pierre. *Realms of Memory: The Construction of the French Past*. New York: Columbia University Press, 2001.

Peele, Jordan, dir. *Get Out*. Universal Pictures, 2017.

Poe, Edgar Allan. *The Narrative of Arthur Gordon Pym of Nantucket, and Related Tales*. Oxford World Classics, 2008.

Poe, Edgar Allan. *Great Tales and Poems of Edgar Allan Poe*. New York: Vintage Classics, 2009.

Otto, Rudolf. *The Idea of the Holy*. London: Oxford University Press, 1977.

Puleo, Risa. "M. Lamar." bombmagazone.org, *Bomb Magazine*, October 8, 2015.

Punter, David and Glennis Byron. *The Gothic*. Blackwell Publishing, 2004.

Radcliffe, Ann. *The Mysteries of Udolpho*. Oxford University Press, 2008.

Radcliffe, Ann. "On the Supernatural in Poetry" *The New Monthly Magazine* 7, 1826, p 145–52.

Rankine, Claudia. "The Condition of Black Life Is One of Mourning." *New York Times Magazine*, June 22, 2015.

Reinhardt, Mark. *Who Speaks for Margaret Garner?* Minneapolis: University of Minnesota Press, 2010.

Riddell CA, Harper S, Cerdá M, Kaufman JS. "Comparison of Rates of Firearm and Nonfirearm Homicide and Suicide in Black and White Non-Hispanic Men." *Annals of Internal Medicine*, May 15, 2018.

Roediger, David R. "And Die in Dixie: Funerals, Death, & Heaven in the Slave Community 1700-1865." *The Massachusetts Review*, vol. 22, no. 1, 1981, p. 163–183.

Ross, Fran. *Oreo*. New York: New Directions, 2015.

Sana Saeed. "The Very Black History of Punk Music." AJ+, 2018.

Sharpe, Christina. *In the Wake: On Blackness and Being*. Durham: Duke University Press, 2016, p. 15.

Southern Mosaic: The John and Ruby Lomax 1939 Southern States Recording Trip, Library of Congress, loc.gov.

Spivack, Caroline, "African-American Graves from 1858 Rediscovered and Restored at Green-Wood." *DNAInfo*, dnainfo.com, August 21, 2017.

Spooner, Catherine. "The Why Factor: Goths." *The Why Factor*, BBC World Service, May 15, 2017.

Spooner, James dir. *Afro-Punk*. Afro-Punk, 2003.

Spracklen, Karl and Beverly. *The Evolution of Goth Culture*. Emerald Publishing Limited, 2018, p. 42-44.

Stanley, Tiffany. "The Disappearance of a Distinctively Black Way to Mourn." *The Atlantic*. Atlantic Media Company, January 26, 2016.

Stowell, William Hendry. *The Eclectic Review*, Volume 6; Volume 24, p. 468.

Taylor, Kate. "The Thorny Path to a National Black Museum." *The New York Times*, January 22, 2011.

Tettenborn, Éva. "Melancholia as Resistance in Contemporary African American Literature" *MELUS*,

Vol. 31, No. 3, Race, Ethnicity, Disability, and Literature, Fall, 2006

Thacker, Eugene. *In the Dust of This Planet: Horror of Philosophy (Volume 1)*. Winchester: Zero Books, 2011.

Triandafyllidis, Nicholas dir. *Screamin' Jay Hawkins: I Put a Spell on Me*. Astra Show Vision and Sound, 2001.

Valance, Hélène. *Nocturne: Night in American Art,1890 – 1917*. New Haven: Yale University Press, 2018, p. 97.

van Elferen, Isabella. *Gothic Music: the Sounds of the Uncanny*. University of Wales Press, 2012.

Varma, Devendra P. *The Gothic Flame*. Russell and Russell, 1957.

Victor, Daniel. "A Woman Said She Saw Burglars. They Were Just Black Airbnb Guests." newyorktimes.com, *New York Times*, May 8, 2018.

Walpole, Horace. *The Castle of Otranto: A Gothic Story*. Oxford University Press, 2014.

Warwick, Alexandra. "Feeling Gothicky", *Gothic Studies*, Volume 9, Number 1, Manchester University Press, May 2007, p. 5-15.

Wester, Maisha. *Don't Let the Drexciya Catch You in Detroit: Afrofuturisms Gothic Underground*. Talk presented at the International Gothic Association Conference, Manchester, UK, August 3, 2018.

Wilkins, Robert L. *Long Road to Hard Truth: The 100-Year Mission to Create the National Museum of African American History and Culture*. Proud Legacy Publishing, Washington, DC, 2016.

Wilson, Mabel O. *Begin with the Past: Building the National Museum of African American Culture*. Smithsonian Institution, Washington D.C., 2016.

Woolfe, Zachary. "A Goth Male Soprano Who Plumbs the Darkness." *New York Times*, January 12, 2017.

Wright, Christina M. "Emmett Till's Casket Headed to Smithsonian," *Associated Press*, August 28, 2009.

Yanuck, Julius. "The Garner Fugitive Slave Case," *The Mississippi Valley Historical Review,* Vol. 40, No. 1 (Jun., 1953), pp. 47-66

Zhao, Christina. "'BBQ Becky,' White Woman Who Called Cops on Black BBQ, 911 Audio Released: 'I'm Really Scared! Come Quick!'" *Newsweek.com*, Newsweek, September 4, 2018.

NOTES

Goth-ish

1   For clarity "Black" is capitalized when discussing race, people, or culture and the lowercase "black" for the color.

2   propagandamagazine-gothic.tumblr.com

3   From Carrie Hawks' short animated film *Black Enuf* (1997).

4   *Post-Punk.com*, "Goth So White? Black Representation in the Post-Punk Scene", 30 November 2017, post-punk.com.

5   Jones, Heather (18 May 2016) "Being Weird and Black Doesn't Mean You're Interested in Being White," *Wear Your Voice*, wearyourvoicemag.com

6   Igadwah, Lynet (18 October 2013) "Gothic fashion taking root" *Nairobi News*. airobinews.nation.co.ke

7   Design by Bianca Xunise for Adorned by Chi.

8   "The Practice of Slavery at Monticello" monticello.org

9   Botting, Fred (1955) *Gothic: The New Critical Idiom*, London: Routledge

10 Groom, Nick (2012) *The Gothic: A Very Short Introduction*, Oxford: OUP

11 While it is extremely tempting, I'm reluctant to use the term "hauntology" when talking about the gothic, a topic which regularly refers to the hauntings of "real" ghosts not metaphoric ones.

Based on a True Story

1   Walpole also coined the term "gloomths," which is to me a more accurate description of the gothic sensibility than goth. If only it wasn't such an unattractive word to pronounce.

2   Yanuck, Julius (June 1953) "The Garner Fugitive Slave Case." *The Mississippi Valley Historical Review*.

3   Bogira, Steve (September 7, 1987) "They Came in Through the Bathroom Mirror: A Murder in the Projects." *Chicago Reader*.

This Spooky Thing Called Slavery

1   Radcliffe, Ann. (1826). "On the Supernatural in Poetry" *The New Monthly Magazine 7*.

2   Bouie, Jamelle, "Black Victims, It Always Is." *Slate Magazine*, Slate.com

3   Bouie, Jamelle (26 Nov. 2014) "Michael Brown Wasn't a Superhuman Demon to Anyone but Darren Wilson." *Slate Magazine*. Slate.com

4   Fry, Gladys-Marie. (1975). *Night Riders in Black History*. The University of North Carolina Press.

Black Is the Color of My True Love's Hair

1   Jackson, Stanley W. (1986) *Melancholia and Depression*, Oxford: OUP

2   Dickey, Colin (2016) *Ghostland: An American History in Haunted Places*, New York: Viking

When Doves Cry

1   Davison, Carol (2017) *The Gothic and Death*, Oxford: OUP
2   Spivack, Caroline, "African-American Graves from 1858 Rediscovered and Restored at Green-Wood"
3   Dunlap, David W. "Evidence of Burial Ground Is Discovered in East Harlem"
4   "The Woman in the Iron Coffin," *Secrets of the Dead*, PBS, 3 October 2018.
5   Laqueur, Thomas W. (2015) *The Work of the Dead: a Cultural History of Mortal Remains*, New York: PUP
6   Delgado, Melvin (2003) *Death at an Early Age and the Urban Scene: The Case for Memorial Murals and Community Healing*, Westport: Praeger Press
7   Cooper, Martha and Sciorra, Joseph (1994) *RIP: Memorial Wall Art*
8   Huyssen, Andreas (2000) "Present Pasts: Media, Politics, Amnesia," *Public Culture*
9   Riddell, Corinne, Harper, Sam Cerdá Magdalena, Kaufman, Jay, "Comparison of Rates of Firearm and Nonfirearm Homicide and Suicide in Black and White Non-Hispanic Men, by U.S. State", *Annals of Internal Medicine*, 15 May 2018.
10 The refrain is repeated with Walter Scott, Jerame Reid, Phillip White, Eric Garner, Trayvon Martin, Sean Bell, Freddie Gray, Aiyana Jones, Sandra Bland, Kimani Gray, John Crawford, Michael Brown, Miriam Carey, Sharonda Singleton, Emmett Till, Tommy Yancy, Jordan Baker, and Amadou Diallo.
11 Roediger, David R. "And Die in Dixie: Funerals, Death, & Heaven in the Slave Community 1700-1865," *The Massachusetts Review*, Spring 1981

12 Rankine, Claudia. "The Condition of Black Life Is One of Mourning." *New York Times Magazine*, June 22, 2015.

13 Nora, Pierre (2001) *Realms of Memory: The Construction of the French Past*, New York: Columbia University Press.

Screaming it to Death

1 The entirety of *Southern Mosaic: The John and Ruby Lomax 1939 Southern States Recording Trip* is available online through The Library of Congress: "This recording trip is an ethnographic field collection that includes nearly seven hundred sound recordings, as well as fieldnotes, dust jackets, and other manuscripts documenting a three-month, 6,502-mile trip through the southern United States. Beginning in Port Aransas, Texas, on 31 March 1939, and ending at the Library of Congress on 14 June 1939."

2 Neal, Larry (1972) "The Ethos of The Blues." *The Black Scholar* 3, no. 10

3 Margolick, David (2001) *Strange Fruit: The Biography of a Song*, New York: Ecco Press

4 Smiley, Tavis (23 October 2017) "My Conversation with Annie Lennox," *Huffington Post*. huffpost.com.

5 "History of Lynchings," NAACP, naacp.org

6 Halperin, Moze. "The Curious History of 'I Put a Spell on You'"

7 McCann, Ian. "I Put a Spell on You brought bliss to all who touched it — except its composer"

8 "The Life of a Song: I Put a Spell on You," (5 February 2017) *FT Life of a Song*. podtail.com.

9   Thompson, Dave and Greene, Jo-Ann (November 1994) "Undead Undead Undead," *A Study of Gothic Subcultures*. gothicsubculture.com

10   Wester, Maisha, *Don't Let the Drexciya Catch You in Detroit: Afrofuturisms Gothic Underground,* paper presented at the International Gothic Association 2018 Conference in Manchester, UK

11   Ketchum, William (15 October 2008) "Mayor Esham? What?", *Detroit Metro Times*. metrotimes.com.

The House on Boston Boulevard

1   Adams, Julia and Schönle, Andreas (2010) *Ruins of Modernity*, Durham: DUP

2   Rueters, (1 November 1994) 'Hundreds of Fires Light Up Devil's Night in Detroit,' *New York Times*.

3   Apel, Dora (2015) *Beautiful Terrible Ruins: Detroit and the Anxiety of Decline*. Rutgers University Press, New Brunswick.

Fear of a Black Planet

1   Ferber, Michael (2010) *Romanticism: A Very Short Introduction*, Oxford: OUP

2   Fisher, Mark (2014) *Ghosts of My Life Writings on Depression, Hauntology and Lost Futures*, London: Verso.

3   The name Melanie is derived from the Greek "melaena," meaning black or dark.

ACKNOWLEDGEMENTS

My deepest gratitude to all the people who gave me their encouragement, their support, their advice and their time: Laina Dawes, Colin Dickey, Griffin Hansbury, Robin Lester Kenton and the folks at Brooklyn Public Library, Marc Owens, Dominic Pettman, T. Cole Rachel, and Eugene Thacker. Thank you to Evan Michelson, Joanna Ebenstein, Laetitia Barbier and The Morbid Anatomy Museum for inspiring me to pursue this in the first place. Special thanks to Bellweather, Fred Berger, Michael Bierut, Theresa Fractale, Haqq & Estevam, Kambriel, M. Lamar, Marko Smiljanic, and Kameelah Janan Rasheed for their generosity and their art. Thank you to Tariq Goddard, Josh Turner, Jonathan Maunder, and Repeater for having faith in me.

Special thanks to my partner in goth Sarah Feinstein for all of the above and more and to my family who've always encouraged me to keep running and stay awake.

Repeater Books

is dedicated to the creation of a new reality. The landscape of twenty-first-century arts and letters is faded and inert, riven by fashionable cynicism, egotistical self-reference and a nostalgia for the recent past. Repeater intends to add its voice to those movements that wish to enter history and assert control over its currents, gathering together scattered and isolated voices with those who have already called for an escape from Capitalist Realism. Our desire is to publish in every sphere and genre, combining vigorous dissent and a pragmatic willingness to succeed where messianic abstraction and quiescent co-option have stalled: abstention is not an option: we are alive and we don't agree.